LIFELONG EDUCATION AND INTERNATIONAL RELATIONS

CROOM HELM SERIES IN INTERNATIONAL ADULT EDUCATION

Edited by Peter Jarvis, University of Surrey
Consultant Editors: Chris Duke and Ettore Gelpi

ADULT EDUCATION IN CHINA
Edited by Carman St John Hunter and Martha McKee Keehn

COMBATTING POVERTY THROUGH ADULT EDUCATION
Chris Duke

LIFELONG EDUCATION AND INTER-NATIONAL RELATIONS

ETTORE GELPI

CROOM HELM
London ● Sydney ● Dover, New Hampshire

Croom Helm Ltd, Provident House, Burrell Row,
Beckenham, Kent BR3 1AT
Croom Helm Australia Pty Ltd, Suite 4, 6th Floor,
64-76 Kippax Street, Surry Hills, NSW 2010, Australia
British Library Cataloguing in Publication Data

Gelpi, Ettore
    Lifelong education and international relations.
    1. Continuing education
    I. Title
    374   LC5215

    ISBN 0-7099-1186-6

Croom Helm, 51 Washington Street,
Dover, New Hampshire, 03820, USA

Library of Congress Cataloging in Publication Data

Gelpi, Ettore.
    Lifelong education and international relations.

    (The Croom Helm series in international adult
education)
    Bibliography: p.
    Includes index.
    1. Continuing education.   2. Adult education.
3. International education.   4. Education – International
cooperation. I. Title. II. Series.
LC5215.G445   1985   374   85-14982
ISBN 0-7099-1186-6

Printed and bound in Great Britain
by Billing & Sons Limited, Worcester.

CONTENTS

Editor's Note

Foreword

Author's Note   1

Part One: Introduction   5

1. Lifelong Education: Concept and Aim   7

2. The Meaning of Life and the Meaning of History in
   Some Contemporary Cultures   17

Part Two: The Economic and the Technological Dynamics   23

3. International Division of Labour, Educational Policies and
   a New International Order   25

4. Mobility of Labour, Technological Changes and the Right
   to Work   45

5. Living Without Wages   61

6. Youth and Adult Workers' Education   71

Part Three: The Search for and the Importance of Culture   81

7. Culture in the City, Rural Environment and Community
   Development   83

8. Migration and Creativities   97

9. Emerging Cultural and Educational Needs   105

**Part Four: Educational Trends and Issues: Examples of Action,
Co-operation and Conflict**   117

10. Towards a New Educational Order: Encounters and
    Confrontation in Education   119

11. Intercultural Co-operation in Higher Education   129

12. The Human Sciences and North-South Relations   141

13. The Educational Implications of Recent Scientific, Techno-
    logical and Cultural Exchanges between Japan and China   149

14. A Personal International Experience   160

15. Creative Struggles for Development   170

16. Lifelong Education: Opportunities and Obstacles   178

End Note   190

Suggested Reading   195

Index   199

EDITOR'S NOTE

The Croom Helm Series in International Adult Education brings to an English-speaking readership a wide overview of developments in the education of adults throughout the world. Books are planned in this series of four different types:

(a) about adult and continuing education in a single country;
(b) having a comparative perspective of two or more countries;
(c) studies having an international perspective;
(d) symposia of papers from different countries having a single theme.

This study is of the third type, written by Ettore Gelpi, whose experience of lifelong education worldwide from his international position has given him a unique perspective upon this phenomenon. Because of this, the book locates education within international social and political systems in a fresh and revealing manner. It is a study that asks questions, queries established ideas, and is profoundly challenging. Yet it is a personal book, written out of concern and understanding and this, perhaps, makes it even more challenging.

Ettore Gelpi is Head of the Lifelong Education Unit at Unesco. He is vice-president of the Sociology of Education Research Committee of the International Sociological Association; founding member of Quale Societa (an association for the study of the problems of the division of labour), Rome; member of the Council of the University of Vincennes in Saint-Denis (Paris), and lecturer at the University of Paris I, Sorbonne and at the Collège Coopératif, Paris.

FOREWORD

I wish to express here my great debt to many friends who helped me in the translation of some chapters and in the revision of some others, particularly to: C. Griffin, P. Jarvis, M. Matsui, J. Rennie, R. Ruddock, D. Singh, J. Smith, R. South.

I am also grateful to other friends, associations and institutions who have included me in their activities and have thus provoked and stimulated my thinking. Hence some of the following chapters have appeared elsewhere, namely: Chapter 1 in *International Encyclopedia of Education* (Pergamon Press, 1985); part of Chapter 7 in *Dialectics and Humanism* (Institute of Philosophy, Warsaw, 1983); Chapter 9 in *Policy and Research in Adult Education* (Dept. of Adult Education, University of Nottingham, 1981); Chapter 10 in the *Scottish Journal of Adult Education* (1984); Chapter 16 in the *International Journal of Lifelong Education* (1984). I am grateful for permission to reproduce these articles in this volume. In addition, I am grateful to Faber & Faber for permission to quote Jordan Burgess Coate's poem from *Hard Lines*.

Ettore Gelpi

AUTHOR'S NOTE

The awareness of the international dimension of education is growing, but relevant information is quite limited. Interdisciplinary work is needed as education is affected by developments in the political, economic, cultural, and social sectors. The dialectical nature of the relations between education and developments in the wider society is often ignored. In this book an attempt is made to avoid pedagogical romanticism or 'diplomatic' language in the exploration of these problems. A new international order of education is advocated as one instrument that can contribute to peaceful and just international relations and to a more meaningful world development.

International educational actors are people working: independently, in educational institutions and in regional and international governmental and non-governmental organisations. Their goals are sometimes opposed, sometimes conflictory, and sometimes complementary and reinforcing. All unidimensional and universalistic interpretations are misleading: realities are much more complex. The merging interest in the international dimensions of education is promising, for, although new fields tend to provoke demagogy and ambiguity, they also lead to the emergence of new energies and hopes.

The French painter Braque wrote that 'Conformism starts with definition'. I think he is right: this book is therefore not a book of definitions. But the reader will likely ask: 'What does lifelong education mean?' Although I will give it a definition, I consider this as other definitions such as those for 'basic needs', 'community', 'popular culture', and other central concepts as only temporary: all active concepts undergo a continuous process of enrichment in terms of interpretation, conception, definition and practice. With this in mind, it is possible to say that lifelong education is at once a concept, a policy, a practice, a process, a goal and an ideal, and that it applies to the whole lifespan of man. Morever, it is an education that can develop anywhere; that occurs both within and outside institutions; that is both formal and non-formal, initial and continuing.

Education is equated with lifelong learning: support for this statements provokes harsh reactions, for in this perspective education becomes a significant and relevant means of transforming social and political life. Are international relations for new forms of domination

1

or perhaps for new forms of liberation? Can education play a role in the struggle for liberation? In the following pages ways for further developing human freedom are explored, along with the obstacles, the blind alleys and objective difficulties associated with activities directed towards liberation. Manipulation in international relations is widespread, and the risk that international 'co-operation' is damaging to the most perceptive researchers in different countries is real. Powerful countries can influence the national policies of the most peripheral countries through the active support, at the international level, either of people who are more docile or who favour their 'line'. Vested interests in the academic world or in governmental and non-governmental international organisations could also lead to the concentration of resources and personnel in irrelevant research topics, and to open and covert opposition to more significant inquiries and activities.

International relations have many dimensions: financial, economic, military, ideological, technological, scientific, cultural and educational. The levels of interdependence and dependence within international relations vary in relation to the power structures operating within and between the countries concerned. Even without their knowledge, international researchers and policy-makers in the field of education could be accomplices to the development and reinforcement of further dependency. On the other hand, they can also help to encourage international creativity and solidarity and to develop more meaningful education and cultural action.

Is it possible to define clearly the theoretical and strategical foundations for a progressive policy in international educational relations? It is easier to be precise about the goals of international educational relations than about universal principles and theories. These goals naturally reflect one's philosophy of life. My own philosophy has been influenced by the various cultures I have had the opportunity to encounter, to study, to live in and to love; and by determined people who have tried and continue to try to improve and transform the conditions of life of oppressed people and social groups across the world. My educational goals have been affected by my prior experiences. I am fighting for a non-dogmatic education that enables people to think by themselves and for themselves about the world around them and their roles within the communities in which they live, love and struggle. Education should be an instrument in social, aesthetic, political and economic struggles that seek to achieve social justice at the national and international level, that helps to develop the creativity of children, youth and adults and, at the same time, empowers them to act upon and transform their world.

But how is such an education to develop? Educational theoret-
icians, educational policy-makers and educators must be sensitive to the
varying cultural, psychological, political and economic dimensions of
life within different countries. Solidarity, democracy, family ties,
engagement, state, universality, nature, individual, mass — all have different meanings for different peoples and social groups because they
reflect their differing practices, conditions, and ways of being and per-
ceiving. We need to carry out sound analyses of the variety of meanings,
but we must not forget that educational creativity is mainly the result
of the social and cultural activities of the people themselves — popular
action is not only dependent upon formal conceptual clarity. It is on
popular action that education moulds itself. International technological
scientific, financial and economic relations influence and change the
framework within which education operates: it is the responsibility of
those engaged in educational activities to find new ways to make education relevant and to reinforce popular participation in local, national
and international affairs. Unfortunately, too often international relations in education are becoming the basis of new vested interests. Sometimes, resistance is the only answer to hollow calls for international co-
operation. Sometimes, contradictions are impossible to solve because
interests are opposed and mediation is hopeless.

Even in such situations, however, there are alternative courses of
action from which to choose: one can remain a passive observer or,
regardless of the moralistic criticisms of others, act to give a concrete
meaning to international relations. Different people and social groups
perceive objective international relations and of their relevance to community life differently, reflecting the wide variations in their concrete
daily experiences.

One can assist them towards new ways of understanding and acting
if one is sensitive to these differences in perception. I support the
development of an education that allows a full use of human resources,
that contributes to meeting individual and collective human needs, that
reinforces mutual understanding and solidarity. Therefore, I struggle
against all forms of racism that limit the full development of human
capacities, against class and bureaucratic social structures that reinforce the conviction there are different levels of human needs in
relation to the hierarchical status differences, and against all forms of
imperialism, old, new and emerging, that impose the will of dominant
groups and countries.

This book is concerned mainly with the relations between economics, culture and education at the international level. It explicitly criticises conceptions of education either as a completely independent or dependent variable in international economic relations, and of intercultural studies that fail to analyse the power structures that operate both within and between countries. The international division of labour, scientific and technological transfers, the ideological nature of commercial, cultural and educational enterprises do exist, and they do need to be analysed from an international perspective. At the same time, struggles against dependency, new forms of co-operation between peoples and countries, research for new foundations in international political life have to be made known and closely explored because they help to generate new educational thinking and practices.

The metaworld of international education is largely irrelevant if research and action become insular, or if it is used to help propagate sectarian ideologies or consumption models. On the other hand, international education could be of great relevance as more and more people have direct experience beyond their own national cultures. Educational curricula are waiting to be opened to the broader world culture. Educators are unsatisfied with narrow national programmes and with their parochial national training.

Are emerging tendencies orientated towards more internationalist or nationalist forms of education? What is preferable? Are tendencies divergent or compatible? Here again, a dialectic approach is needed. False internationalist ideals could transmit and impose new dependencies and national, cultural and educational identifications could be the means of opening up certain countries to the world.

An internationally oriented education is not easier to achieve than a nationally oriented education, and yet the international activity is multiplying.

Would it be possible to make this activity relevant to the building of an international democracy that allows peoples and social groups to be respected regardless of their level of economic development, their military strength, their race, social status or their worldviews?

PART ONE: INTRODUCTION

1   LIFELONG EDUCATION: CONCEPT AND AIM

There has always been lifelong education for some social groups. Whether it will become an instrument of liberation for all, or an instrument of domination for a few is not yet decided. It has many obstacles to overcome; the existing forms of education are very resistant to change. There are, however, numerous pressures for a wider opening of educational opportunity, and from experience in places throughout the world, it is possible to identify the problems it must face and the way in which it may go.

There is no universally accepted concept of education, and the same applies to the development of the concept of lifelong education. Educational ideologies have been and are closely linked on one hand to social and economic factors, and on the other to political, religious and social ideologies. Lifelong education, as expressed by different civilisations, reflects the specificity of those civilisations and their cultural traditions. The Greek *paideia*, the European Renaissance and the Age of Enlightenment are not the only reference points of lifelong education. The original African communities have contributed to the socialisation of education and thus to its permanence in the social realm.[1] One could find several examples of this kind in different civilisations and different countries.

The concept of lifelong education at the end of the nineteenth century and in the twentieth has found new definitions and practices related to 'struggle' situations, to industrialisation and post-industrialisation, to international thinking and action, to more profound research into history and comparative education, to rediscovery of the cultural and educational identity of countries which have newly gained their independence.

Instrument of Liberation or Domination?

In many countries the history of education has not been examined from the viewpoint of the people[2] because external domination has been imposed through foreign educational values, suppressing educational and cultural traditions.[3] Within contemporary societies and international co-operation, however, the history of lifelong education

7

cannot escape the question, 'Is it an instrument of liberation or of domination?'[4]

The spread of the right to education at the level of nation and social class during, for example, industrial revolution, decolonisation, social struggle, has not always meant emancipation and education for all, or education of some quality for those who receive it. It is often one-dimensional in that it is education for production, for good citizenship, or for the integration of the immigrant worker;[5] for the inculcation of religious, political and consumer ideologies. The international division of labour, the result of the universalisation of markets, has often widened the gaps in formal education between social groups and between countries. Consequently, it has affected the educational systems of countries and the educational paths of individuals. In certain industrialised countries the tendency is towards the universalisation of higher secondary education and even of the first level of higher education; in others, for example certain developing countries, illiteracy still persists.

It is perhaps the complexity of lifelong education as a goal, policy, concept, practice, process, and particularly the dialectical relationship between these elements, which make lifelong education living rather than reified. Reification is in fact the great risk of lifelong education, because it means a schooling of society. Yet its basis will not be in the school, but in the much more global phenomenon of a structured lifelong education.

The confusion between lifelong education in society and the often enclosed world of its specialists leads, according to some views, to a limited and false vision of lifelong education in contemporary societies. Educational professionals are often seen as accomplices of power in reducing the cultural and educational creativity of the masses. Pedagogical discussion in its moralising, prophetic, futurological expressions often elaborates its own abstraction, and the practices of educational institutions seem to resist all changes. Perhaps, through what lifelong education for all has to say about policies and educational activities, the idea of struggle will appear in the educational field.

There is the struggle to give meaning to lifelong education as there have always been struggles in schooling: schooling or lifelong education for discovering creativity and developing the individual; schooling or lifelong education for domestication and manipulation? The path from the concept of lifelong education to its realisation is characterised by struggles in social life and educational institutions in such areas as: the type of relationship between formal and non-formal education, i.e.

dialectic or dependent; the contribution of such non-teaching educators as cultural, social and political movements to educational activities; criteria for assessing the effectiveness of the educational system, both internally and externally; the extent to which self-directed learning is encouraged, especially that of a collective nature.

Struggles go on in different countries, chiefly with a view to democratising or to reproducing social structures through education. Democrations and reproduction[6] are everywhere a basic theme of the educational debate. Lifelong education has been presented as a new route for spreading democracy, but often the realisation of this concept has once again meant the reinforcement of the existing social structure. Mere quantitative expansion of education and culture does necessarily result in the creation of democracy. To think of democratising while retaining the same goals, teachers and curricular content is either to be naïve or manipulatory, but in any case it is a hopeless enterprise. The relationship between culture and education often encounters obstacles and engenders anxieties, posing the question whether one may expect educational experiences to evolve from formal training to enquiry, from direction to discovery, and from boredom to pleasure.

Education for All

The emergence of new publics, the expansion of leisure time and the increase in the number of educational premises reflect the possibility of education for all; it could occur from earliest childhood to old age at work or in leisure, in the school or in the community. But these changes often cause disquiet to those in power since they neither control this expansion nor its emergence. On the one hand, there is a reinforcement of the formal educational system (often in response to public demand), and on the other there is overt or hidden repression of spontaneous educational and cultural demonstrations. The contradictions between living culture and the contents of schooling are at the root of increased educational demand and at the heart of the crises in educational institutions, particularly in industrialised countries.

The Copernican-type of revolution in education, of education for all and by all, disconcerts the professionals of initial and continuing education, but educational demand lies, perhaps, in this direction. The young who have to repeat a year of school get bored and leave; apprentices, future production workers or unemployed, who simply reject vocational training; adult education which often manages to disillusion for the second time those who remember bitterly their initial educational experience – these are only some examples of the failure of an education which provides no opportunity for creativity, research, production, nor individual or collective self-education. By contrast, courageous experiments have been and are taking place in formal and non-formal education to meet the new educational and cultural demands, and these experiments show that educational innovation and creativity are possible – in the cradle, the school, the university and in daily life.

The Transformation of the Labour Market

The crisis and transformation of the labour market through the progress and universal application of technology and at the same time an explosion of non-skilled work, which demands either very high or virtually no qualifications, are at the root of present and future changes in educational systems. But these changes are not automatic. Educational systems often endeavour to preserve educational patterns which no longer fulfil the functions asked of them, while social and cultural forces seek to reproduce educational and cultural activity.

The implications for educational policies and activities of the international division of labour are also obvious in the segmentation of the labour market, the spread of technology, the multinationalisation of financial and industrial capital, emigration at continental and intercontinental level, and the concentration of scientific and technological research in certain countries. In economies which are more and more interdependent; and bound by old and new international and social divisions of labour, progressive educational projects can only be plans for struggle in the concrete and often unfair conditions of life. Education can be granted or demanded. In each case the meaning and the quality of education will be different.

Education – an Instrument of Social Policy

Education must form a part of any society's plan of domination, liberation and construction. In history imperial plans have often been imposed by educational models. The idyllic mask of education tends to be blurred, but often a Manichean interpretation follows. It is indeed difficult to comprehend the dialectic dimension of education.[8]

Educational plans develop in a situation of contradiction between the concept of lifelong education and the continuation of apartheid, colonialism, racism, lack of intellectual freedom, physical violence; and the worst is the use of lifelong education to mask the violence inflicted by man upon man in order to tame his fellows. When the educational structures are opened up in new places, at new times and to new publics they are often confronted by the inertia of bureaucratic apparatuses incapable of resolving the problems of personnel and maintenance. These educational structures have often found support in clubs and societies in their efforts to widen access. It is expressed through groups of parents, neighbours, workers, young people and among the artists, researchers, scientists and creative workers.

Lifelong Education in Educational Practice

Examples of the intellectual and practical development of lifelong education are increasingly to be found in educational policy and practice, as for example in:

- the development of international economic relations, the international division of labour and their consequences for educational policies;
- the search for a coherent education, with alternative models for development;
- the search for the historical origins of lifelong education in different civilisations;
- lifelong education as a plan for comprehensive change in educational policies and systems;
- lifelong education as a response to the search for new values in education;
- lifelong education as a social project to transform educational and productive structures;
- the organisation of territory (decentralisation, community participation, grass-roots initiatives) and of education;
- lifelong education and organisation of educational time (sandwich courses, recurrent education, courses in firms, introduction of productive work, sabbatical paid leave);
- education and self-learning by means of the mass media in all aspects of everyday life;
- the calling into question of educational institutions and their opening up to the outside world (universities, schools,

libraries, museums);
- relations between formal and non-formal education, by integration, linking, dialectic and/or conflictory relations;
- lifelong education, facilitation and cultural action;
- the inter-cultural links and lifelong education (migrant workers, international training programmes, international schools, foreign study grants);
- lifelong education through art and any other expression of sensory and aesthetic life;
- the search for new ways in initial and lifelong vocational training: the integration of general and vocational education.

The Future of Lifelong Education

The linking or the partitioning of the structure of formal and non-formal, initial and continuing, vocational and general, institutional or self-directed education is and will be the result of educational policies which favour or check the participation of populations in the definition and administration of educational structures. The scarcity or abundance of the education on offer may be at the heart of conflicting situations concerning educational structures, because of unsatisfied educational demands or of insufficient public support. The scarcity of qualified educators for new publics may also be a root cause of policies which seek to join together diverse and unlinkable forms of education.

To 'school' non-formal education, or to 'deschool' the school may hold attractions for some people, but the demand is for both formal and non-formal educational structures, open to a population of all ages. Institutions regularly devoted to research and education may guarantee a progression of content and forms of learning. Social or productive life, cultural life and leisure may express new aims, contents and forms of 'the educational act'. The variety of educational places and times may transform the relationship between teachers and learners, the teacher no longer being the pawn of power, nor the demiurge, but rather one of the actors and a member of the public, who takes part with the learners in the search for, creation of, and transmission of knowledge.

It is difficult to foresee how lifelong education may develop. The expansion of educational time and the multiplication of educational places, whether as a spontaneous social fact or as a deliberate choice of educational institutions and the world of work, may spark off the transformation, or decline, of existing educational structures or the birth of new ones. Some may be valid, while others may be more artificial. Policies and activities of lifelong learning may continue to develop because of: increase in the educational demand and supply; collective demands expressed by workers with a mind to individual and collective education; the crisis in the educational function of the family in some societies and the pressure by parents for better opportunities for their own children; the time exposed to mass communication, the geographical mobility of a great number of workers and also their mobility within the different structures of production; the alternation between education, work, under-employment, unemployment and the transformation and transfer of technologies; the increase in the average lifespan of the individual and the ageing of a significant part of the population; the rapid change of roles within social life; the explosive growth of certain cultural interests.

But the gap between educational institutions and educational and cultural demand is not easy to eliminate. The development of human resources appears to be an answer to the problems posed in individual countries and in international life, but it is also apparent that educational structures tend to reproduction and are often insensitive to the emergence of new publics and new demands. The social, economic and cultural division between individuals and between countries which belong to one or the other section of the labour market, and which take part unequally in the international division of labour, grows wider and goes beyond traditional social classes.[9] Educational institutions face a dualism of production at national and international level. They can reinforce this dualism by ignoring it, or they may recognise it and contribute to its elimination by facing real and other dramatic issues, such as unemployment, lowering of housing standards, loss of liberty, drugs, prostitution, racism, and by integrating them in everyday educational activity.

Today's and tomorrow's society, characterised by rapid demographic growth in a number of countries, by speed of often one-way communication, by forms of lifestyle radically different in different countries and different social classes, faces the challenge of educating for complexity. Confronted by this complexity all education may perhaps be transformed into lifelong education, and a new order of education may appear necessary, involving the whole of the population, and making a positive discrimination in favour of particular social groups, ethnic minorities, and the most underprivileged populations and countries.[10]

Practical Tasks

Among the tasks envisaged there will be:

- The involvement of the widest possible representation of the people in the management of educational systems with open access to all the necessary information in order to perform the function effectively. The widest possible education of the entire population with the opportunity for them to acquire information about the most complex tasks of contemporary societies regarding production, social and cultural life.
- The realisation of educational reforms centred on new relationships between the social system, the production system and social and cultural movements.
- The experimentation and development of educational structures capable of satisfying the demands both of particular publics and of the whole of the population, and capable of being a meeting place between traditional and modern education, formal and non-formal education, institutional education and self-directed learning.
- The utilisation of 'space' in, for example, educational institutions, workplaces, daily social life, and time and leisure, to encourage individual and collective self-directed learning and the creation of new knowledge and understanding.
- The association of creative workers in different aspects of educational activity, from the perfection of educational methods and contents to their diffusion by means of mass media and teaching.
- Initial and continuing education of educators in liaison with research, creative and productive activities.
- The definition of methods and contents aiming at individual and collective fulfilment; full intellectual, manual, sensory, aesthetic, linguistic expression; psychological self and interpersonal equilibrium; identification with living, creative culture.
- Establishment of schemes for the evaluation (chiefly educational) of knowledge acquisition, with more attention to the development of individuals and societies than to the mere internal coherence of educational institutions.

The dialectic between social forces and between them and educational and cultural institutions is and will be the basis for the implementation of or failure of the tasks indicated above. A new national and international order of education where education may be lifelong, and creative for everybody, disdaining every form of domination and indoctrination, is an objective yet to be attained. It is, perhaps, nearer today than in the past, but its achievement is no less difficult for the men and women who are committed to it.

The Actors

Is lifelong education going to create further dependence or more independence in international relations? Is lifelong education leading towards international democracy or towards a new colonialism? In the world of tomorrow, will lifelong education provide an adequate response to the growing demand for education from individuals and peoples caught up in the reality of the contradictions of everyday life? A dialectic approach is needed. Teaching people how to live with these contradictions is perhaps the principal task of education today. Education which is but an adaptation of education limited to strictly professional ends will no longer satisfy the individual, the community or the countries of the world called upon, often at very short notice, to face up to radical changes affecting economic, social and cultural life.

Who will be responsible for initiating policies and activities to further lifelong education? Individuals, the creative members of society, social and cultural organisations, professional educators — all will have a part to play, whether in educational institutions, at the place of work, in the social life of the community, or in the field of leisure. Everyone, whether professional educator or not, will have to contribute to the formulation of policies, legislation, renewal, administration and the evaluation of education. Furthermore, it will be for those principally involved in the educational process, whether children, adolescents or adults, to define the objectives, the philosophy and the values of education. Those involved in the educational process are becoming more numerous, and present a challenge to which existing educational and productive systems have been reluctant to respond.

Lifelong education means making full use of a society's human resources. It is an education which meets individual and collective aspirations and needs and whose end is action. It is in the search for this full use of human resources that education stands revealed as the sensitive nerve point in the relations between the social classes, between 'central' and 'peripheral' countries and between individuals fighting for individual and collective human rights against the forces of repression.

Notes

1. J. Ki Zerbo, *Histoire générale de l'Afrique —I: Méthodologie et préhistoire africaine*, Paris, Stock-Unesco, 1980, pp. 782-3.

2. B. Suchodolski, *Projet pour une histoire universelle de l'éducation*, Warsaw, 1982

3. E. Mochida, 'A Critique of Modern Education With Special Reference to The East,' *International Journal of Lifelong Education*, no. 1, 1983

4. P. Freire, *Educaciòn y cambio* (Education and Change), Buenòs Aires, Ed. Busqueda, 1976

5. S. N'Dongo, *Exil, connais pas*, Paris, Cerf, 1976

6. A. Meier, *The Role of Education in the Transformation and Reproduction of the Class Structure in Socialist Societies*, Tenth World Congress on Sociology, 1982

7. Z. Zuda, *Divorce of Educational Goals and Career Aspirations?* Tenth World Congress on Sociology, 1982

8. Li Kejing, 'Is Education a Superstructure or a Productive Force?' *Social Sciences in China*, no. 3, 1980

9. S. Majstorovic, *Kultura i democratija* (Culture and Democracy), Belgrade, Prosveta, 1978. F. Jeanson, *L'action culturelle dans la cité*, Paris, Seuil, 1973

10. C. Bonanni, *Education for Human Needs*, New Delhi, Indian Adult Education Association, 1982

2 THE MEANING OF LIFE AND THE MEANING OF HISTORY IN SOME CONTEMPORARY CULTURES

For the first time in our history, different cultures are communicating, or have the opportunity of communicating substantially because of transcontinental migration, communication facilities and the fact that cultures coexist in the same city, village or family. These communication processes are often very difficult and take a long time to be learned (this process is in itself a cultural development). Respect fo other cultures facilitates communication between peoples, countries and within the countries themselves; the possible evolution of culture is related to the complete expression of individual cultures and their openness to other cultures.

The emergence of previously repressed civilisations and cultures along with the continued overt suppression of minority groups, the hidden manipulation through the mass media of local and national cutures, all assume new significance and meaning in our planetary and often consumer societies. Explosive contradictions exist; people are frequently both the subject and the object of cultural repression. Industrialised countries compete with developing countries, one age-group with another, local workers with migrants, urban workers with semi-urban and rural workers — these conflicts are often of a cultural, rather than simply of an economic nature.

The building up of their own history is for many peoples, social groups and ethnic minorities a need — a need which can sometimes be realised, and which sometimes requires a struggle if the goal is to be achieved. The appraisal of its own history and identity necessitates the full use of the nation's own cultures and the possibility for cultural, technical and scientific interchanges of a more equal nature at local, national and international levels.

A dominant culture sometimes ignores, downgrades or represses a minority and/or peripheral culture; cultures thus tend to hide those of their values related to life, to history, to their way of interpreting time and to the use of space.

The denial of another culture is not only a kind of self-defence, but also a result of psychological prejudice. The difficulty a nation has in mastering its own culture encourages reaction against other cultures.

17

The existence and expansion of national languages and, in some cases, the reintroduction of these languages by ethnic groups in a country will facilitate an appraisal of the nation's own history, and give it the possibility to view differently a past obscured by external and/or internal colonial, economic and/or ideological domination.

The re-appropriation of culture can, in some cases, as a first reaction, lead to various types of cultural immobility, but this is usually only temporary. Regaining linguistic and cultural confidence can enable people and countries to acquire rapidly a more open attitude towards other histories, cultures and societies.

The culture of daily life, of institutions, of communities: these three aspects each assume a different significance in modern societies. In industrial societies the culture of the community is weakening; the culture of daily life and that of many bureaucratic institutions interact more or less dialectically. Development models (ideology, economic constraints, choice of investments, etc.) which are imposed influence cultural development through the output of the mass media and publishing houses, through patterns of vocational training and through having cultural models other than the indigenous culture.

The history and the study of one's physical environment is still part of many contemporary cultures, but has disappeared in others, even though some efforts have been made to rediscover this domain.

The exploitation of popular and folk culture is quite a new trend. We speak of the protection of folklore, but we are witnesses to several violations of this both from an economic and a cultural point of view. Traditional medicine, ways of life, arts, crafts, music and dance are moving more and more from the so-called 'developing' countries to industrialised societies. Often, however, these changing traditions lose their meaning because of their rapid commercialisation. In addition, the tourist's appreciation of local traditional culture in many countries has resulted in the creation and consumption of 'secondhand' arts and crafts.

The demise of folklore is taking place because of competition with the commercial and ideological culture transmitted by the mass media. The desire and taste for individual and collective production of a local culture has been lost in many modern schools simply because individual consumption models have been introduced, sometimes through the mass media and sometimes the pressures generated by the need to produce and sell commodities.

New cultures are emerging from very ancient ones in a dialectical manner. Cultural identity needs to find new ways of reacting to external influences or unidimensional internal developments. New emergent cultures are often misunderstood because dominant civilisations prefer to represent them as either very traditional or as new, very unidimensional methods of development.

The meaning and significance of history is now changing due to the promotion of the importance of cultural identity, which has stimulated ethnical and historical identity. We are today witnesses of the revival of cultural identity, through the re-introduction of the mother-tongue and the partial re-appropriation of historical materials lost during colonial and post-colonial economic and political domination. At the same time, these new resurgent cultures are confronted with the new computer sciences at both national and international levels. On the one hand, nations identify themselves with their own history and, on the other, have to learn formal computer language in order to overcome distances and facilitate communication. Electronic memories are improving the human memory. Positive and negative aspects go hand in hand: the positive aspect is that of the possibility of keeping a record of different cultural, historical and contemporary events; the negative side is that the dominant culture will be the one which has most control and knowledge of these new sciences.

Modern education and modern culture are influenced by different variables: the world of work, cultural and social tradition, the international division of labour, the autonomy or the dependence of the modernisation process and the initiative of social movements. The meaning of time and history can be influenced by these variables.

The segmentation of the labour market has a strong impact on the living conditions of workers in many countries, so that cultural identity and solidarity among workers in industry are sometimes lacking. New patterns of working life have a strong influence on the daily life of people. The productive and consumption processes of the life of urban industrial workers have become increasingly separated from their imaginative and creative activities; they have separate cultures at home, in the factory, during the weekend, in social life and in high cultural and educational activities. The amount of satisfaction and job fulfilment gained during working hours is related to the worker's choice of leisure activities and social life. Individual and collective needs for manual work, creative work, social recognition and satisfaction within the community and the need for physical recreation often result in different cultural patterns in the life of the same person. The coexistence of different cultures in the same country, village or family is, in fact, new to our present-day society. The same person can have a full social and cultural life at his place of work; be culturally conservative and narrow minded within his family and social life and in the community; yet he may have an ideology of internationalism.

It is becoming more and more difficult to express and represent the meaning of life in today's society through philosophical categories. Philosophical schools of thought seem to have disappeared, as modern philosophies seem no longer able to give moral, aesthetical, or theoretical interpretations of our life. On the one hand, philosophies of daily life are presently emerging, and, on the other hand, there is still a search for philosophies that provide a basis for understanding and expressing new values.

The marginalisation of less-privileged workers, the separation of groups of workers in relation to special incomes or fields or professional competence, and new forms of individual leisure are all dividing the working classes in many countries. This has serious consequences since workers' solidarity is essential for the transformation of the social relation in the world of work and the development of mutual understanding, human dignity, and fellowship. Instead of acknowledging these new trends, working-class organisations (trade unions, political parties, cultural associations, etc.) sometimes ignore them. The result is weakness in the face of an invading commercial culture, the rapid development of new and largely superfluous consumer needs and the impoverishment or demise of a new creative people's culture.

The intellectual, who is sympathetic to and sometimes actively supports working-class aims, finds himself ill at ease in some specifically working-class organisations and institutions when these constrain his intellectual creativity. At the same time, intellectuals in their daily work as professors, researchers writers and artists, lose the habit of collective practice. In either situation a more creative and effective alternative is to work within institutional constraints, always keeping in mind larger objectives to be achieved.

In some cases, and during certain periods in the history of each country, public institutions patronise new progressive cultural and educational activities. These cultural and educational policies lead to new forms of participation by the people in the management of educational and cultural institutions; they promote new cultural activities in the arts and sciences — a positive answer to growing educational and cultural demands. These activities result from popular attempts to overcome immediate crises, while at the same time people try to live meaningful lives.

Cultural life is not a separate world: artists involved in cultural activities cannot alone change the world, but they can contribute to the invention and formal representation of new ideas, new methods of expression and new indicators of human development. The fight for culture and political independence in many countries is a positive cultural sign: the accessibility of meaningful cultural activities to an increasing number of people is another positive indicator. Paradoxically, the contribution of people to education and to the creation of cultural products has been both enlarged from an instrumental point of view (since more people receive formal education); and reduced (since people have no opportunity to contribute to the most relevant modern educational and cultural contents and processes, i.e. the mass media). Therefore, it is sometimes true that, for example, the traditional peasant, deprived of or having only a limited formal education, has a meaningful culture, whilst the more educated urban qualified intellectual, technician or skilled worker, often has problems of cultural identity.

Culture is an important dimension of development. Over the last few years industrialised countries have not, generally speaking, increased cultural investments all that rapidly. Nevertheless, many people are beginning to realise that an increase in cultural activities may be one of the keypoints for human survival. Less economically privileged countries are becoming more and more aware that a dynamically oriented cultural identity is an important instrument for international recognition.

PART TWO: THE ECONOMIC AND THE
TECHNOLOGICAL DYNAMICS

3 INTERNATIONAL DIVISION OF LABOUR, EDUCATIONAL POLICIES AND A NEW INTERNATIONAL ORDER

The International Division of Labour

Today, the international division of labour (IDL) is essentially different from that prevailing during the nineteenth and at the beginning of the twentieth centuries. Formerly, the division of labour was

> based on the exchange of primary commodities coming from the Third World with commodities exported by industrialized countries.
>
> In contrast the international division of labour which is developing today is based on the exchange of popular consumer goods manufactured by abundant and cheap manpower in developing countries with more sophisticated goods mainly incorporating capital and an advanced technology from the older industrialized countries.[1]

Within the marginal countries agricultural production is geared particularly to external rather than internal consumption: subsistence production has given way to the production of cash crops that are only indirectly profitable to the peasants who produce them. New centres of industrialisation are being created in continents other than Europe and North America. At the same time, the industrialised countries are also undergoing changes, with some regions within these countries even experiencing the effects of 'de-industrialisation'.

It must be kept in mind that all generalisations made to distinguish between different groups of countries or between different countries within given groups, according to economic, ideological, geographic or cultural characteristics, are superficial to the extent that they do not take into account the specificities of individual countries. Most typologies used to distinguish the different categories of countries on the international scene are primarily inspired by economic considerations: 'developed countries', 'developing countries', 'newly industrialised countries', 'planned economies', 'oil-exporting developing countries', etc. Yet countries are also distinguishable according to their social, educational, cultural, scientific and technological dimensions, the specific characteristics of which do not necessarily reflect their different levels of economic development. Although statistics provide relevant information, the picture which they present does not always correspond exactly to reality. Most statistics do not take into consideration, for example, the non-formal labour market, non-money exchanges, transactions mediated through third parties, and, above all, the wide disparities within economic, political, social, individual countries.

> The incorporation of sociological assumptions into the construction of economic models would enable greater recognition to be given to the problem of power. Because the environment studied by economists consists of agents of unequal strength, a political economy relevant to contemporary society becomes part of the scientific study of power.[2]

Studies of existing power structures should not limit themselves to national contexts, for:

> The struggle for social transformation is not confined to each society and country, because societies are linked in an international system of exploitation which profits a power structure based largely in the industrialized world though not without annexes in the previously colonized countries. Ruling elites of most societies are both accomplices and rivals at the same time. Exploitative relationships exist within most countries and are largely sustained by the exploitative system that cuts across frontiers.[3]

The new IDL is often imposed on countries and not usually negotiated, limiting the possibility of implementing 'independent' development policies. The transformation of the international labour market conditions the implementation of economic reforms which ought to be the instruments of these policies. The global context of decisions concerning the marginal nations often makes development projects dependent on variables (military, political ideological, energy, etc.) which are not always positively related to the development objectives of the countries in question.

Theorising about development in marginal nations requires consideration of the nature of independency, based upon the imperatives of the international economic markets and the possibilities of negation that are open to developing countries. In response to the present economic, political, and social crises within many of the industrialised societies, alternative criteria and strategies of development are being sought by both the developing and industrialised countries.

Newly industrialised countries and those in the process of industrialising often find themselves faced with an anguishing dilemma: either to participate in the IDL as it presently stands and suffer the consequences of low profit margins, the over-exploitation of human labour, inadequate control over the movement of capital, dependence on external technologies, or else risk the hardships and uncertainties of self-sufficiency. To take part in the new IDL in the context of one's own development policy is the ideal objective, but it is a goal that is difficult to achieve.

The analysis of the behaviour and experiences of marginal nations faced with the IDL shows that ideological stances and structure of political systems are perhaps less determinative than the nature of the relation of these countries to the international market. It is a country's bargaining strength which affects its ability to structure its relations with the governmental, financial and commercial institutions of other countries to its own advantage. A country's bargaining strength is determined primarily by the size of its internal market, its degree of mastery over technological developments, the nature of its national resources, and, perhaps most importantly, by its geopolitical position.

The IDL is dynamic: it reflects the political and economic dynamics of the international balance of power. It is both cause and effect of phenomena such as the great rural-urban, continental and intercontinental migrations, the nature of exchange, the transformation of the processes of production, transformation of investment in technology, and the conditions of child, youth and adult employment. The IDL, moreover, implies different consequences for different groups of countries.

In industrialised countries the IDL more often creates a concentration of industrialisation, fundamental and applied research, employment with trade union and social protection, and compatibility between the culture of the nation and the world of work. In developing countries, however, the almost total lack of funds for fundamental and applied research and the lack of trade union and professional safeguards for workers are often associated with high levels of unemployment and underemployment, with emigration, and, in certain cases, with the dispossession of entire populations, with imported processes of production and technology without local control, and with a large element of non-formal and temporary employment.

The new IDL has consequences for the relations between social classes within different societies. Often, the concentration of decision-making powers in the hands of a small minority in the state apparatus reinforces the position of elites living in the capital. In many cases, existing liberties within marginal nations have been weakened. Even so, although many authoritarian regimes have been concerned only with the profitability of workers as labour power, it must not be forgotten that other regimes have been successful in negotiating their position within the new IDL and, at the same time, have defended their independence. For the moment, at least, the IDL does not contribute to raising questions about the causes of the great disparities in the relations between given population sectors and their relative shares of national and international incomes.

Table 3.1: Per cent Distribution of World's Total Output (1980)[4]

	% of world population	% of total output
Developed countries	25	79
Low-income countries	47	5

As reflected in Table 3.1 'even allowing for distortions due to income and price differences between countries, the general conclusion is inescapable that much of the world's output is produced and consumed by relatively few of its people'.[5] Such an assessment must not lose sight of the fact that such production is often at the expense of underprivileged peoples and countries; their contributions of physical labour and precious natural resources are undervalued, and their sacrifices of time, health, and life are rarely included as forms of output.

Even though the quality of life is not necessarily reflected in the level of Gross Domestic Product (GDP) *per capita*, the striking differences that exist between levels of GDP at the extremes are indicative of great disparities between the conditions of life of the peoples within different countries. In the developing countries, where the majority of the world's population lives, the average GDP *per capita* is US $650. As seen in Table 3.2, even within this group of countries some are much better off than others: the low-income countries of Asia and African have *per capita* GDPs below US $300.

The great disparity in rates of economic growth even among the developing countries is clearly illustrated in Table 3.3. While the GDPs of a few countries have experienced high rates of increase (e.g. 5.2 per cent in the case of countries of south and east Asia), in an increasing

Table 3.2: Population, GDP and GDP *per capita* in 1980, and Growth Rates 1960-83[6]

Country group	1980 GDP (billions US$)	1980 population (millions)	1980 GDP per capita (US$)	GDP growth rates (average annual percentage change)					
				1960-73	1973-9	1980	1981	1982	1983[a]
Developing countries[b]	2,118	3,280	650	6.3	5.2	2.5	2.4	1.9	1.0
Low-income	549	2,175	250	5.6	4.8	5.9	4.8	5.2	4.7
Asia	497	1,971	250	5.9	5.2	6.3	5.2	5.6	5.1
China	284	980	290	8.5	5.7	6.1	4.8	7.3	5.1
India	162	675	240	3.6	4.3	6.9	5.7	2.9	5.4
Africa	52	204	250	3.5	2.1	1.3	1.2	0.5	-0.1
Middle-income oil importers	915	611	1,500	6.3	5.6	4.3	0.9	0.7	0.3
East Asia and Pacific	204	183	1,110	8.2	8.6	3.6	6.7	4.2	6.4
Middle East and North Africa	28	35	800	5.2	3.0	4.2	-2.4	5.5	2.0
Sub-Saharan Africa[c]	37	60	610	5.6	3.7	5.5	3.9	1.1	0.3
Southern Europe	201	91	2,210	6.7	5.0	1.5	2.3	0.7	-0.9
Latin America and Caribbean	445	241	1,840	5.6	5.0	5.8	-2.3	-0.4	-2.2
Middle-income oil exporters[d]	654	494	1,320	6.9	4.9	-2.4	2.4	0.9	-1.7
High-income oil exporters	228	16	14,250	10.7	7.7	7.4	0.0	–	–
Industrial market economies	7,463	715	10,440	4.9	2.8	1.3	1.3	-0.5	2.3

Notes: – Not available.
a. Estimated.
b. Data for 1982 and 1983 are based on a sample of ninety developing countries.
c. Does not include South Africa.
d. The estimated 1983 data exclude Angola, the Islamic Republic of Iran, and Iraq.

number of countries the rate of growth of GDP has been negligible and even negative.

Table 3.3: Developing Countries: Percentage Rates of Growth of GDP,[a] 1979-83[7]

Regions and country groupings	1979	1980	1981	1982	1983[b]
Africa	4.8	1.9	-1.0	0.5	1.0
South and East Asia	2.5	6.0	6.6	3.5	5.2
Western Asia	6.0	-2.9	-1.1	-0.5	-3.1
Western hemisphere	6.5	5.3	0.7	-1.4	-2.8
Mediterranean[c]	2.9	1.2	2.6	2.5	1.8
All developing countries	5.0	3.2	1.6	0.5	—
Capital-importing developing countries	4.7	4.8	2.6	0.8	0.7
Least developed countries	2.4	2.3	1.2	1.5	2.0
Memorandum item: frequency distribution of GDP growth rates for 83 countries					
Zero or below	10	17	30	32	40
0.1-2.5	8	12	11	22	12
2.6-5.0	28	25	16	18	17
5.1-7.5	20	12	12	9	9
7.6 or over	17	17	14	2	5

Source: Department of International Economic and Social Affairs of the United Nations Secretariat, based on national and international sources.
Notes: a. The data for the regional groups are aggregated with weights based on constant 1980 prices and exchange rates.
b. Preliminary estimates.
c. Cyprus, Malta, Turkey and Yugoslavia.

The IDL, rather than being the result of negotiations between countries of the centre and those of the marginal, is primarily the consequence of competition or agreements between industrialised countries. The intense competition between industrialised counries, separately or between groups of countries (EEC, Japan, USA and, in a certain way, COMECON) is not new, but it is growing.

With respect to industrial production, the IDL tends to accentuate the process of differentiation between the relative shares of developing countries in worldwide industrial production: Africa 2.3 per cent (without considering Zimbabwe, North Africa, South Africa); East Asia between 64 and 68 per cent; Latin America between 21 and 26 per cent; cent; South Asia between 7 and 11 per cent; the Middle East and North Africa 5 to 6 per cent.[8]

The 'de-industrialisation' of Africa may appear as a paradox, but it has been noted, in certain countries of the region, that there has been a withdrawal of industrial investment; events occur as if Africa carries no weight in East-West or North-South relations, except as a strategic area either for military purposes or as a source of raw materials. For the developing countries in general, however, it is estimated that they will increase their share in world industrial production from 11 per cent (1970) to 28 per cent (2000) as well as their share in world trade in manufactured goods from 12 per cent (1970) to 27 per cent (2000); at the same time, this increase will be somewhat offset by the parallel increase in their percentage share of the world's population from 70 per cent (1970) to 78 per cent (2000).[9]

In the future, the volume of international trade is also expected to increase rapidly. By 1990 trade may well expand at a pace almost twice as fast as the growth in world output. In 1980 23 per cent of that output was traded; by 1990 it could reach 30 per cent.[10]

It is likely that the developing countries' exports of commodities will grow at a considerably lower rate, which means that those economies that depend primarily on commodities for their export earnings will have to turn to other strategies to boost income for their development needs. The probability too, is that the newly industrializing countries will supply a much larger share of the traditional manufactured goods to the older industrial nations of Western Europe and North America. To compensate for the loss of this portion of their domestic markets, these nations are likely to give greater emphasis to products of high technology. Indeed technological advance is likely to be a principal source of these societies' future manufacturing growth, with the new silicon-chip technologies and the overall explosion in the information and data processing industries perhaps leading the way.[11]

Multinational firms heavily influence international trade between the marginal countries and the industrialised ones; nation states and local industries have limited power in the negotiation with the multinational firms and, in general, the expansion of trade does not necessarily benefit the masses.

The emerging international division of labour will likely serve to increase international and national migrations toward urban and industrial centres. At the same time, harsher competition in the development and marketing of technology will develop in the already industrialised countries. Because of the relevance of this technology for both developing and newly industrialised countries, there will also be increased competition among these latter countries to attract, keep and attempt to master new technologies. Therefore, in all countries, education will be of increased relevance; namely, as far as training, mastering (in the case of transfers of technology) and production of technology are concerned.

The current distribution of research and development (R & D) activities does not promise in the near future any changes in the status of countries that are now producers and consumers of new technologies and those that are primarily consumers of these technologies. In 1974, of the 3,111,800 scientists and engineers employed in the world in R & D, 91.3 per cent were employed in the developed countries. In 1980, of a total of 3,756,100 scientists and engineers employed in R & D, 89.4 per cent were employed in developed countries. In 1974 96.3 per cent and in 1980 94 per cent were disbursed in developed countries on R & D.[12] The flow of highly qualified migrant workers to Europe and North America serves to further reinforce present patterns of R & D: it has been estimated that in the early 1970s 420,000 highly qualified migrant workers were working in Europe and North America.[13]

The IDL itself both reflects and reinforces existing political and military cleavages. Currently, international relations are heavily influenced by the arms-race. The latter not only deepens economic recession by increasing the government deficits of industrialised countries and encouraging strict financial and industrial and commercial policies, but it also bears disproportionately on the Third World. The latter is at increasing risk from outright intervention by the superpowers. Its military expenditures have risen faster on the whole than those of the industrial north. It is clear that neither the arms race nor the recession can be controlled without a major reordering of the present international anarchy.[14] And the present tendency is toward a significant increase in the level of military expenditure.[15]

The new IDL has consequences for social relations and the organisation of the state. Often, because of lack of autonomy, technological and economic dependency, and the consequent alteration of social relation, states become powerless and overly rigid, and allow for only limited forms of participation, initiative and control by their own people. The greater or lesser degree of openness of state structures shows itself in the relations between the state and the people in their places of work, in their homes and in their leisure activities, etc. The creation and evolution of existing states both have implications for educational systems as the latter are often closely linked to the maintenance and reproduction of elite classes and larger social structures. Given that different types of societies have different conceptions of educational requirements and that needs differ, it would be interesting to compare the actual educational theories and educational systems of different countries with the ideologies that lead to action in the political, economic and cultural spheres within those countries. The debate regarding learning and lifelong education could be refined and acquire a new meaning if it were recognised as an area in which ideologically based definitions of educational needs confront each other.[16]

Greater co-operation and collaboration in international relations, on a basis of mutual respect, would, in the long run, be beneficial to all the parties concerned. As an example, greater South-South relations could be beneficial to the South *and* to the North:

> The North stands to gain from successful cooperation among developing countries. The selective promotion of reciprocal trade would give rise to occasional conflicts of interest in specific sectors, but the feedback effects from the development of the South should benefit the growth of the North. In addition, the elimination of the syndrome of financial collapse in the South should reduce the North's fears of recession.[17]

Although desirable, such South-South co-operation, even on a limited basis, is still rare.

New South-South relations seem to be a prerequisite for the development of many countries of the South. Should North-South relations improve, a better co-operation between southern countries would help both the northern and southern hemispheres. Possible areas of co-operation among the southern countries are abundant at the bilateral, subregional, regional, and interregional levels: finance, industry, trade, transportation, distribution. South-South co-operation is becoming a must for southern economies.[18] These options would be attainable if new social relations are developed and if a full use of human resources is achieved.

One can ask whether the North-South dialogue is worth saving; 'without reforms, the answer is no: the result would only be repetition of inflated expectations, counterfeit agreements, and increased cynicism'[19] But what are the relevant reforms? Certainly not the 'stabilisation programmes' or trade-dependent development strategies, as 'stabilisation programmes are most unlikely to be distributionally neutral, which adds to their political sensitivity . . . In general, a country faced with an unenviable payment deficit must reduce consumption or investment relative to income'.[20] In the long run trade-dependent development strategies are often associated with rising national deficits. This has serious political implications as access to needed finance is not without cost. Either way it is usually the less privileged classes that are asked to sacrifice.

Implications of the International Division of Labour for Education

The relations between the IDL and educational policies is not always recognised within research undertaken by comparative educationists; often, generalisations are hasty and misleading as they draw conclusions about structures that are similar in form but not always in function. With respect to the new IDL, the problem of education is raised in a very specific manner within each country and within each social group. Relatively stable educational sytems corresponded to the former IDL in which dynamism resulted from social conflict and/or periods of intense economic development. Today, the functions expected of education in different countries are both proliferating and changing rapidly: training schemes for the unemployed, intensive retraining for certain categories of workers, training without hope of future prospects, providing qualification for migrant workers, etc. To a certain extent, the new IDL brings into question certain aspects of the social division of labour that are based on traditional social-class divisions. Changing labour-force structures are both affected by and affect the changing economic and educational structures within developing countries.

In general, countries of the developing world (Table 3.4) are experiencing a reduction of their agricultural sector which has been associated with an expansion in both their industrial and service sectors. It is important to note that the rate, qualitative nature and implication of these statistics are different for the poorer or richer countries of the Third World: as an example, the expansion of the tertiary sector can reflect either the objective creation of necessary sources or the absence of jobs in agriculture and industry and/or the existence of an over-large bureaucracy.

As seen in Table 3.5, as far as the industrialised countries are concerned, they are also experiencing a decrease in their agricultural sectors. However, this decrease is associated only with an expansion of

Table 3.4: Labour-force Structure: Developing Regions, 1960-80[21] (in percentage)

Group	Agriculture		Industry		Services	
	1960	1980	1960	1980	1960	1980
All developing countries	72.6	59.1	12.8	19.9	14.5	21.0
Latin America and Caribbean(low-income countries)	63.5	49.3	14.8	19.8	21.7	30.9
Latin America and Caribbean (middle-income countries)	45.6	31.8	20.7	25.8	33.6	42.4
China	74.8	60.0	15.4	25.8	9.8	14.2
India	74.0	62.2	11.3	17.2	14.7	20.6
Asia (other low-income countries)	76.4	65.5	8.1	11.8	15.5	22.7
Asia (middle-income countries)	68.0	52.5	12.2	19.4	19.8	28.1
Africa and Middle East (low-income countries)	87.6	80.0	5.1	8.6	7.3	11.4
Africa and Middle East (middle-income countries)	69.8	55.6	12.2	19.0	18.0	25.4
Africa and Middle East (capital surplus oil producers)	68.8	51.8	11.2	18.3	20.0	29.9

Source: Figures for 1960: ILO *Labour Force Estimates and Projections* (Geneva, 1977). Figures for 1980 were estimated on the basis of the trends for 1960 to 1970 at country level.

their services sector, with the industrial sector experiencing an actual decrease in growth. In contrast to the predominant experience within the developing world, this expansion of the services sector in most cases reflects the transformation of the economies of the industrial countries into profitable service economies.

Table 3.5: Percentage Changes in Productive-sector Shares of Total Employment (1970-80)[22]

	Agriculture	Industry	Services
Federal Rep. of Germany	-2.6	-4.6	+7.1
France	-4.9	-3.7	+8.6
Italy	-5.6	-1.6	+7.3
United Kingdom	-0.6	-6.6	+7.2

Because of these changes, there is increasing demand for formal and non-formal educational programmes. But often, financial constraints result in limited access to educational programmes for large sectors of the population (Table 3.6).

Table 3.6: Enrolment Ratios and Literacy Rates (1960, 1970 and More Recent Estimations (MRE))[23]

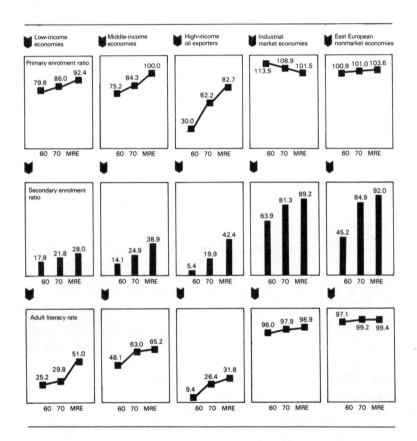

Independence in educational matters is closely tied to cultural creativity and to popular participation in defining and implementing educational policies and practices. The struggle to enrich and defend one's cultural identity is also a better means for workers to negotiate wage levels and working conditions and for marginal countries to negotiate for their role in the IDL.

The contradiction between formal educational systems and the reality of production becomes more and more dramatic as, increasingly, basically agricultural countries or basically industrialised countries are no longer able to make decisions regarding investment, finance and production policies. In addition to the reproductive logic inherent in formal educational systems, there is the impossibility for educational planners to foresee the evolution of educational demand by the labour market. This is not surprising, as economic planners cannot forecast economic development with any degree of precision either.

Interaction between the social system, the productive system and the educational system exists in the history of all societies, but the nature of these influences varies in different countries and at different times during their histories. The most serious problem for many marginal countries is the low level of autonomy of the productive system, which, among other consequences entails: (a) difficulty in developing a coherent national policy for the training of highly qualified manpower; (b) schooling as a response to demand or social pressure, without the perspectives and outlooks consistently required to enable the country to develop global development objectives; (c) frequent reinforcement of private schooling when a democratic project for the state school system brings social stratification into question; (d) difficulties for the state and the national production system to develop a coherent system of vocational training; (e) the expansion of non-formal education, which is largely dependent on foreign institutions (in the economic, religious, political and social areas).

The economic IDL is accompanied by educational measures which tend to reinforce dependence by the marginal nations at an economic and ideological level. Evidently, in international educational exchange, it is very difficult to prevent a movement from the centre. Hardware, software, technical assistance in the area of training only follow one direction, even when it is evident that such imported training does not correspond to the development of underdeveloped nations and that these countries also have a relevant contribution to make.

The transfer of people and their culture from marginal countries towards the centre are largely a loss for the former, taking away the intellectual and physical wealth of people in their youth and adult-hood, without corresponding significant economic advantages.

The educational implications within the IDL of educational policies of the group of market-economy countries (OECD and EEC) and planned-economy countries (COMECON) are interesting to analyse. The concentration of higher research institutions in the most powerful countries within these economic groups makes the less industrialised countries their dependants, with a role limited to industrial manu-facturing, but they are also partially exposed to competition with developing countries. The relations between the arms industry, research and level of education also deserve to be analysed, especially with respect to the reinforcement of the dependence of certain countries within these homogeneous economic groups. The consequences for education of this IDL which concern market-economy countries and the socialist international division of labour are found particularly in higher education, some of which is not available in industrialised and non-industrialised marginal countries because, in some fields (especially tied to high-technology industries, data-processing and the military industry) certain forms of higher education are concentrated in the most economically and militarily powerful countries. These exceptional economic, military and educational powers reinforce the strength of power elites (at the economic, political and administrative level), groups which tend to reproduce themselves by using, among other means, existing educational structures.

On the one hand, it would be interesting to analyse the conse-quences of the IDL on educational systems; and on the other, to see the possibilities of arriving at objectives of educational reform while taking the reality of the IDL into account.

In industrialised countries, the consequences of the IDL are the seg-mentation of the labour market, the social division of workers, the increase of sectors related to scientific and technological research, the progressive disappearance of several industries with low profit margins and, in certain cases, the development of an unofficial employment mar-ket. For education, that means the development of research centres and very advanced higher education where there is the maximum concentra-tion of high-technology industries and above all the R & D sector; a high level of unemployed and underemployed (unemployment and under-employment, visible or hidden according to the specific characteristics of societies); intensive retraining for a part of the population; socio-cultural activity intended to guarantee balance, and lack of unrest with among those made marginal in the labour market (unemployed youth, women, early-retired, etc.); increased vocational training for immigrant workers and the provision of short-term work; transfer of men and technologies in marginal countries.

For the developing countries, the economic pressure on educational systems signifies the supply of a higher number of qualified workers compared with demand, which in turn implies low salary levels, a massive development of short in-service training schemes and training which is added to already long hours of work. The constant increase in the level of education becomes one of the conditions of the economic development of these countries, but this increase in no way signifies democratisation of the society.

In the most impoverished developing countries, the exceptional cost of maintaining children and young people in school (the majority of the population being under 22 years old) leads irresistibly to illiteracy for a significant proportion of the child population. Thus, an obstacle to the full future use of human resources is created. Participation in economic production by the entire school population might encourage the spread of literacy because these children and young people might thus be able to earn sufficient to supply their basic material needs while learning. Alternating study and work is one of the keys to educational reforms in marginal countries and not only in those of the centre; the only fundamental difference is that, in peripheral countries, the work of the great majority belongs to the non-formal sector of production and alternation appears more difficult when associated with this sector.

Collective savings and productive investment (private and public) in the largest sense (agriculture, industry, services, R & D) are the condition for creating employment and for reinforcing the possibilities of negotiating the IDL. Agricultural and industrial policies which favour production, rather than property ownership and the reproduction of social classes, need to be associated with courageous training policies for the entire population (producers, consumers, co-operativists, individual and collective savers, etc.).

With respect to safeguards for workers in marginal countries, it has been difficult for trade unions to become strong enough to defend the workers: often the trade unions of the countries of the centre have imposed methods and strategies on the periphery which have helped reinforce the cleavage between different categories of workers; a common training for young and adult workers would encourage respect for all workers, and not for just a few of them.

Between the continuation of traditional agricultural techniques and those forms which are imposed upon the developing societies, new plans could be prepared that would encourage the modernisation of agriculture. This might be achieved with the help of the peasant masses. But both agrarian and informal technological innovation demand a great amount of vocational training.

The existing educational structures are often inadequate to encourage initiative and autonomy in production; educators who are not potential teachers are isolated from the schools, whose teaching methods and syllabuses are invariably unsuited to the task of improving the creative and productive capacities of children and young people.

Training to strengthen national productive capacity in marginal countries has often been conceived as accelerated vocational training; but the principal educational problem is not this training. It is a matter of re-examining all the content and methods of education, principally with respect to higher education, in order to associate them with the global objectives of these societies. An educational policy which will allow for the full use of human resources and will slow down the drain and under-utilisation of qualified manpower in marginal societies is an educational response to the present IDL.

The implementation of major research programmes − including educational research − is a strategy which, at present, is rarely adopted in the poorer countries. Research appears as a luxury, while it is in fact a necessary condition for development. It is, therefore, important to create structures that encourage fundamental and applied research. The complementarity of research-programme objectives and development objectives of a country is always the condition for preventing research structures, such as those of higher education, from becoming an instrument for reinforcing the power of elites and/or, at the same time, dependence on foreign powers.

In an operational perspective, it is difficult to make suggestions on educational matters. It would be more useful to summarise a series of themes on which work might be undertaken. The new IDL poses problems to the educational systems in both their formal and informal dimensions in relation to: the diffusion of technology; the spreading of training schemes; impact on local languages and cultures; the development of individual and collective independent learning; the migrations of the educated and of educators, the complementarity between education and work; the implementation of educational reforms in marginal countries; the evolution of relevant vocational training; the development of education not dependent on the structure of knowledge from developed societies; the dependence of educational systems of marginal countries on external aid; the nature of educational responses to the progressive segmentation of the labour market; difficulties in the definition of the contents of the formal educational system; the level of demand, and nature of the response to educational and cultural needs; and the character of work and leisure activities, etc. This set of themes applies in different ways to different countries, social classes and age groups, but in one way or another, all educational systems are affected by the new IDL.

The history of theories of the international division of labour continues to be written, and the examination of its general evolution or of its recent evolution cannot yet permit a realistic general conclusion to be drawn.[24]

Education and the New World Order

The new world order, as well as the new international order of education, is at once a concrete objective and an ideal to be attained. The transition from the old to the new order appears to be both difficult and contradictory since the development toward the new world order is not strictly a linear one.

Locating the problems of knowledge and education within this international context is useful for a better understanding of the relationship between education and the new world order. Today the production of knowledge in international economic relations is of central importance to the economic life of most countries in all four sectors of production — agriculture, industry, services and R & D. The production and the transfer of knowledge are among the most powerful instruments of new relations of domination or equality.

Currently, initial scholastic education is having a reduced impact in the face of education transmitted by the media. At the same time, broader conceptions of education are emerging which have come to include notions of a continuous education linked to productive activities as well as the acceptance, at the conceptual and sometimes practical level, of an approach to education that is relevant to all times and places. From this enlarged perspective of education, the impact of education for the new world order cannot be ignored.

The recovery by a country of its educational identity occurs through a reappropriation of its educational and cultural history. The history of education is part of the heritage of all peoples, but is not always available in a written form. To know and live one's educational history as it becomes formalised or to write that history when it has not yet been codified, also contributes to the construction of a new international order of education on a foundation of greater equity.

Creativity emerges as one of the most powerful instruments of both individuals and peoples who direct their own education. It allows young and adult learner-educators to come to know their own culture, to create educational means both for defending themselves from commercial educational and cultural influences and to control technological and educational diffusion in order to encourage development in their own countries. It is because of the risks associated with creativity in educational matters that the degree to which it is allowed to individuals and social groups in educational institutions is closely linked to their relative power in national and international social hierarchies. In effect, education based on creativity in the important centres of research and higher education is concerned with the training of elites, especially those of the most powerful countries: in contrast, highly structured and controlled forms of education are directed toward populations whose proper 'moulding' is the true educational goal.

Intercultural and intereducative relations, often regarded as necessary to the success of a new order of education, can be both ambiguous and full of contradictions. The emerging elites of the marginal countries are not always representative of their own people. By subtle means and biased educational systems, powerful groups in centre countries can reinforce, and even create, their own systems in marginal countries. The rapid increase in the level of demand for training in international co-operation has stimulated the most powerful centre countries to establish, sometimes with the help of the Third World countries, contacts in education and the media which will permit them, through more indirect means, to continue to exercise an educational and cultural control of the most marginal societies.

This perhaps pessimistic analysis of international relations in the sphere of education, should not hide the fact that human creativity is dynamic and capable of frustrating the schemes of those who seek to impose new forms of imperialism through educational means.

Luckily, the history of mankind has never been written in advance, and the history of education is no exception. In the past imprisonment of opponents to established regimes has contributed to the training of future political leaders, periods of 'reflection' in detention camps endured by scientists have often preceded successful research careers; the weapons of war have been turned against their oppressors, used by those against whom they were directed — both as instruments of defence and as workshops for scientific technological education. History is full of surprises which enable men to be confident in their future. All this is paradoxical, but still cultural and educational exchanges between countries and between peoples are desirable, through peaceful, creative and constructive means.

A leadership that is often manipulated does not exclude the possibility of research or the creation of humanism that is: anti-racist; sensitive to the different forms of human creativity; concerned with the individual and collective rights of men with respect to their objective and subjective existences; and, above all, active in the creation of an international society.

The new world order is closely associated with the construction of this new humanism, which will develop through often desperate struggles for respect for human dignity against the direct or indirect physical and moral violence inflicted on humanity. Struggle and non-violence should not appear as antithetical modes of action but, on the contrary, as equally necessary means for creating social contexts within which human creativity and dignity will be reinforced.

Notes

1. A. Griebine, *La nouvelle économie internationale*, Paris, PUF, 1980
2. B. Burkitt, 'The Contemporary Crisis in Economic Thought – a Radical Analysis', *The Indian Economic Journal*, Jan.-Mar. 1980, p. 124
3. P. Van Rensburg, *Looking Forward from Serowe*, Gaborone (Botswana), The Foundation of Education with Production, 1984
4. World Bank, *World Development Report*, Oxford, Oxford University Press, 1984, p. 6.
5. Ibid., p. 6
6. Ibid., p. 11
7. United Nations, *World Economic Survey*, New York, 1984
8. B. Kadar, 'La participation croissante des pays en développement à la division internationale du travail industriel', *Industrie et développement*, no 3, 1980
9. OECD, *Interfutures analysis*, Paris, 1979
10. A.W. Clausen, *Global Interdependence in the 1980s*, Washington, World Bank, 1983
11. Ibid.
12. Unesco, 'Estimated World Resources for Research and Experimental Development, 1970-1980-1984'
13. V. CNUCED, *Technologie: aspects du transfert inverse de technologies relatifs au développement*, Manilla, 1979
14. L. Luckham, 'Militarization and the New International Anarchy', *Third World Quarterly*, April 1984
15. M.T. Klare, 'Arming Elites: the Role of Militarism' in *Ties that Bind*, R. Clark, P. Swift (eds), Toronto, Between the Lines, 1982

16. R. Ruddock, *Ideologies – Five Exploratory Lectures*, Manchester, The University, 1981, p. 81

17. United Nations, *Overcoming Economic Disorder*, New York, Department of International Economic and Social Affairs, 1983

18. G. Martner, 'Rôle de la coopération régionale dans le cadre de la stratégie globale de la coopération entre pays du tiers-monde', *Revue Tiers-Monde*, Oct.-Dec. 1983, p. 756

19. R.L. Rothstein, 'Is the North-South Dialogue Worth Saving?' *Third World Quarterly*, January 1984

20. T. Killick (director and editor), *The Question for Economic Mobilisation: the IMF and the Third World*, London, Heinemann, 1984

21. ILO, *World Labour Report*, 1984

22. P. Perulli and B. Trentin (eds), *Il sindacato nella recessione*, Bari, De Donato, 1983, p. 15

23. World Bank, *World Tables*, 1984, p. 145

24. M. Humbert, 'Evolution récente des théories de la division internationale du travail', *Revue d'économie industrielle*, no. 14, 4ème trimestre 1980, p. 41

Various authors, 'Education permanente et division internationale du travail', *Education et société*, no. 6, April-May 1984

4 MOBILITY OF LABOUR, TECHNOLOGICAL CHANGES AND THE RIGHT TO WORK

The Cultural Characteristics of Work

Work and the relations of people to work are not only to be regarded as having only economic or social dimensions but cultural as well. The absence of a national identity in a country also has consequences for the content and the quality of work, the characteristics of which affect the creativity of both producers and consumers.[1]

If, therefore, the cultural and social dimensions are fundamental to our thinking about work, it is important to remember that the evolution of work, of unemployment, of production and consumption within each country and also in relation to the world economy are becoming more and more decisive, not only within production but also in its financing and commercialisation.

The Dynamics of International Economic Relations

The reciprocal relations between the three 'worlds' are characterised, above all, by their specificity: generalisations such as those that will be proposed are thus only indicative of probable tendencies and not deterministic statements. The First World, which is composed of industrialised societies with market economies, such as Europe, Japan, the United States and Canada, is today experiencing severe competition between its various constituent members in the sphere of foreign economic relations. The Second World, composed of the industrialised countries with planned economies is today, because of strong internal pressure for greater imports, generally an exporter of raw materials and energy to the First World for the sake of foreign-exchange revenues. The Third World (especially the countries of the Pacific around Japan, Brazil, Algeria, etc.) nowadays experiences very different realities from those of the countries which are the most industrially developed. They also experience serious financial debt. Within the Third World the factors of impoverishment, de-industrialisation and the enforced agricultural production for the external market are destroying countries whose economies were already precarious. These very different realities stem from the state of result of the labour market and the demand that workers make upon the labour market itself.

The relations between the First and Second Worlds and the Third World are characterised by new forms of dependence in economic, technological and military terms. There is massive emigration from the Third World to the First World, but also from one Third World society to another. This involves the loss of both unqualified and highly qualified workers for these countries.

The Transformation of International Relations

The internationalisation of the world economy[2] has consequences for the geographical mobility of workers and for the plight of Third World countries, which seem merely to be victims of that mobility.

The increasing world scale of the economy and consequent circulation of workers requires a transformation of international relations on the basis of greater international justice. Political de-colonisation is not sufficient unless accompanied by economic de-colonisation. From dependence to interdependence: this process requires a democratisation of internationl financial, economic and commercial structures (World Bank, IMF, GATT), increased co-operation between the Third World countries, and international trade between countries which is linked to some form of training.[3]

The mobility of capital also has consequences for the mobility of technology and of workers. It is also interesting to note that

> capital is relatively autonomous according to the degree to which states favour development. The interests of transnational groups do not necessarily coincide with those of states, and frequently countries adopt development objectives without playing the game of dependent specialisation, so that other countries are therefore continually subject to the international division of labour.[4]

Geographical Mobility

In many countries the geographical mobility of workers continues, therefore, to increase in different ways. The most significant emigrations and immigration, in fact, occur both between and within the Third World countries themselves. This geographical mobility is reinforced by the growing number of refugees, whose numbers exceed 10 millions. Often economic emigration and political emigration are linked.

The slowing down of economic growth in the industrialised countries has curbed their immigration, without however blocking it; for migrant workers continue to occupy low-status jobs which nationals do not want for themselves, performing services which the national internal labour market cannot adequately supply, and constituting an important reserve for supplying the future requirements of the labour market.

Even though immigration has been slowed down, immigrant labour is always present in the industrialised societies, particularly since the arrival of immigrants' families, which often indicates that the wives of immigrant workers enter the labour market, and thereafter the second generation. In the industrialised countries, now in the course of restricting immigration, the control of the entry of migrant workers is being replaced by policies of repatriation, assimilation and integration.[5] These policies, in turn, have consequences for the mobility of workers and, as a result, for their families as well.

One of the implications of the mobility of workers is the possibility for new intercultural relations between the national and foreign workers inside a given country. Policies for work and education which do not take into account this intercultural dimension effectively ignore the benefits resulting from the availability of a range of human resources. Intercultural relations provide an opportunity for cultural exchange as long as this is in two directions: the contribution of migrant workers is equally as valuable as that of national workers.

Technological Change and Immigration

The technological changes in production are responsible for a decrease in the movement of migrant workers, especially in European countries; but

the foreign population and foreign workers continue to grow in numbers because of the arrival of their families and the consequent natural increase, and also because an increasing proportion of young people and women from abroad are seeking employment. This tendency will be accentuated in the years to come, and it is one of the reasons why those countries concerned should intensify their efforts to achieve the social and economic integration of these groups.[6]

Migrant workers will be affected by the restructuring of the world economy but

> the restructuring of an economy in crisis continues to impose a new rationality in the short and the long term on the labour market affecting both the national and the foreign workforce in respect of: innovation and new technologies and the declining birth-rate in the developed countries.[7]

The bargaining position of the Third World countries on geographical mobility is weak. On the one hand, the governments of those countries have a limited power and, in some cases, a limited will to negotiate. On the other hand, the countries which receive migrant workers benefit from a situation of an 'abundance' of labour. The weak unionisation of migrant workers on arrival in the country and during the early years of migrant work, is another reason for the limited opportunities for collective bargaining.

Professional Mobility

The geographical mobility of workers and the professional mobility of individuals occurs in a number of different ways such as: 'simply changing employer; moving from one economic sector to another; from textile to automobile industry without changing profession; in short the change of jobs.'[8] Workers are experiencing different types of mobility: that chosen in the course of individual or collective promotion or a better quality of life; that imposed by technological change and/or the law of quick profits; mobility that merely occurs as one progresses along the career path — in a sense one is carried along by the progress of the events. In this third case, workers are interested in educating and preparing themselves to cope with, anticipate and plan for different types of mobility.

The mobilty of labour, over time, in its legal aspects (temporary, part-time, fixed-term contracts)[9] involves only a particular section of the population of a country, women, the young and migrant workers.

The mobility of workers and its nature are influenced by the limited choice before Third World countries between policies based mainly upon investment on the part of industrialised countries, and those based mainly upon the spread of technology to the Third World countries.[10]

The Organisation of Work and Mobility

The strategy of automation is above all a strategy for the organisation of work. Indeed,

> in other words, a strategy of automation even considered in its most technical aspects (characteristics of hardware, conceptions of software) constitutes a strategy for the organisation of work. Information technology, which represents a whole range of possibilities for organising activities resulting from scientific and technological development, is rich in possibilities for combination. Televisual technology can displace activities which today are concentrated in offices, and change the social conditions of work.[11]

Automation could also result from the claims of workers to better working conditions.

> The Swedish advances in robotics are largely due to action by trade unions against production-line work. This example may be generalised: the computerization of many third-level services, fully assumed by the staff, has not run into much resistance. It is known in effect that those professions which have traditionally had control over their own instruments of work (farmers for example!) are much more receptive to the introduction of computer science.[12]

Furthermore, due to the technological transformation of work marginalised groups begin to struggle for equal rights.

Mobility and organisation within the system of production is related to social class and the nature of the economic process; indeed, it is impossible to conceive of some mobility in terms of productive activity without changes in the class structure.[13] Naturally, the two structures interact with each other, and it is obvious that belonging to one social class or another strongly affects the possibility of access to one or another productive activity.

A redistribution of the social and international division of labour could have important consequences for the mobility of labour within societies and between countries, but we are only now beginning to consider the application of a democratic theory of the division of labour.[14]

Mobility and Information

The mobility of work and workers through the processes of information deserves attention. On the one hand, the concentration of information in certain countries is creating jobs; on the other, the information process makes possible the displacement of technologies and of job creation.[15]

'The utmost development of technology simultaneously makes possible both a universal humanity, in this new iron age, and its apocalyptic destruction.'[16] The father of cybernetics, N. Wiener, has also reminded us of the changes which would be necessary in order to make the second industrial revolution beneficial to mankind:

The first revolution replaced the power of the human arm with that of the machine. The modern industrial revolution, in a similar way, is destined to replace the human brain . . . Of course, just as the qualified carpenter, the professional mechanic and the good dressmaker have survived to some extent the first industrial revolution, so the reputable expert and the capable administrator could survive the second. Yet if the second revolution were to be accomplished, the human being of average ability, or even less, would not have very much to offer which would be valued in terms of money or in terms of what could be disposed of in the market. The obvious answer is that it is necessary to base society upon human values which would not be those of the market place.[17]

The increased productive output of machines is accompanied by a decline in other elements of the ecosystem:

The critical factors are therefore three in number: demographic pressure, the growing differences in wealth distribution and energy policies which constantly tend to convert greater and greater amounts of energy (in order to increase the output of work) . . . Only the output of human labour is increased, whilst the earth itself diminishes in terms of its energy, metals and seas.[18]

A new synthesis is apparently necessary for understanding the relations between Utopia, technology and education.[19]

Automation and the Right to Work

The implications of new technologies on the labour market have not yet been adequately explored. Often we exaggerate the possibility of transforming most of our jobs into highly sophisticated ones; in the USA, while jobs for computer systems analysts will increase over 100 per cent between 1978 and 1990, yet only 200,000 new jobs will be created. In contrast, there will be over 600,000 new jobs for janitors and sextons.[20] The coexistence of high technology job categories and non-skilled jobs categories will accentuate their disparate nature.

> One of the important aspects of new technologies, and notably of micro-electronics, informatics, robotics, new materials and new energies, is their horizontal diffusion into many productive activities. The introduction of these new technologies provides an excellent opportunity to modernise and rejuvenate traditional sectors at the production, management and marketing levels.[21]

But what would be the cost to the workers? 'Technology is not the kind of variable that can be isolated, nor does it have the kind of dimension of such classic factors or production as capital and labour.[22] This is one of the most important reasons why it is difficult to make any kind of reasonable forecast on the subject. Everybody agrees that during the past two centuries basic technological innovations have been associated with long-running cycles of economic activity.'[23] But what about the next economic cycle?

Mobility resulting from new technologies could lead to stable employment in certain instances. The conclusions of a Japanese report concerning the consequences of micro-electronics for employment indicate that

> the number of jobs will mainly be increased among the operators of computer controlled machine-tools and diminish among foundry-workers. This perfectly illustrates the problem of qualifications posed by the new technology: an unemployed foundry-worker has little chance of being able to adapt to the role of an operator of computerised machines.[24]

But the relation between automation and job-creation remains contro-versial: on the one hand it is clear that there is a decline in the number of workers taken on and a loss of employment through the introduc-tion of automation, on the other it is clear that automation increases productivity – a necessary condition for improving employment pros-pects.[25]

Thus, the right to work appears as an extension of the rights of citi-zenship and equality: this proposition is founded upon considerations which are not only ethical but economic as well. What is proposed is a transfer of resources, today being used to keep workers in unemploy-ment, towards keeping them in occupation. For example, in 1981, in the United Kingdom, the cost of unemployment was £3,400 per person without taking into account all the costs of medical services, which, in general, are much higher for those who find themselves un-employed.[26]

Proposals for the universal right to work are not at the moment very firmly included in the employment policies of many industrialised societies. In the era of the Welfare State, the state took over the costs of unemployment: recent trends are more in the direction of relieving the state of these functions and of reducing the taxation which went towards maintaining the Welfare State, leading to an increase in the number of unemployed and thus to the denial of a universal right to work. From the social right to work to a universal right of individuals to work – this transition, at the centre of the debate, is still far from being realised.

New technologies can contribute not only to the organisational needs of the productive system, but also to the individual and collective needs of personal and social life. A different appraisal of new technologies can reorient technological research in this direction. They can transform educational and leisure life, they can enrich the non-working time of many categories of people and increase the learning opportun-ities of the people. 'The slogan might then become "Computing Power to the People". In a way, this parallels an earlier technological devel-opment, namely the printing-press which, by reducing communication costs, increased the potential for democratic practices'.[27]

The Creation of Employment and Demand for Socio-cultural Services

The right to work produces a number of consequences the main one being the new forms of solidarity amongst wage-earners – those who experience the division of labour and the resulting differentiation in their wages. But it is also linked to the creation of new jobs, which are greatly needed both by the industrialised societies because of the imbalances in their development, and by Third World societies since they are a condition for their development.

In the case of the industrialised societies there are some cultural, medical and, to a certain extent, social and educational services which are still inadequate and very much lagging behind the needs of a modern society. Nevertheless, there are an increasing number of private services available to the better-off, and even to the less well-off. Often, in the case of the Third World societies, the minimum level of basic infrastructures has not been attained, a fact which tends to block their development. Rising demand and the differentiation of social, educational and cultural services requires mobility on the part of workers in the public services in order to respond to increasing social, cultural and educational needs. There is a possibility of conflict between the rights of workers responsible for these services and those of the workers who use them. The response might be one of mobility, related to demand, accompanied by policies of training and guaranteed employment.

Another response in terms of work might perhaps be a strategy based on the 'reduction of working-hours, part-time work, paid educational leave, guaranteed minimum wage, the development of significant activities for the unemployed without loss of benefits or allowances and of projects financed for the unemployed.'[28]

Industrial Democracy and Mobility

Industrial democracy has appeared as an interesting development in several countries,[29] which looks at the relations between development and industrial democracy on the one hand, and between automation and the situation of a country within the international division of labour, on the other. Does a privileged situation within the international division of labour, and a high level of automated production create favourable conditions for an industrial democracy? Does it contribute in some degree to the mobility of workers? To what extent does a privileged situation within the internatonal division of labour and the existence of industrial conflict put some countries ahead of others in the matter of industrial democracy?

Widespread mobility of workers, especially in countries where trade unions are weak and social classes relatively unstructured, in times of economic crisis leads to frequent alternation as between work, unemployment, training, underemployment, requalification and dequalification.

The average period of unemployment experienced by young people varies from one industrialised country to another. To a certain extent it is inversely proportional to the power of trade unions, so that in the case of workers whose employment is being defended by their unions there is greater protection of those with something to lose and rigidity towards those who need to gain employment. This acknowledgement has led some unions to pose the problem of unemployment more in terms of the workforce as a whole and not just of those who are actually in work.

Knowledge, Education and Mobility

A major revolution in productive activity is brought about by the fact that the production of knowledge and the spread of learning and training are themselves becoming major productive activities. In this way mobility is bound up with the production of knowledge. To conceive of mobility in this way does not mean that its causes have to be accepted in these terms, but only to acknowledge certain of its characteristics. Work, linked with geographical and professional mobility, chosen or imposed, requires social and cultural qualifications and not just professional ones. The social relations of production influence the technology of production and vice versa,[30] and mobility is affected by technological and social relations. Hence, the need for workers to understand technological and scientific developments in the workplace.

This mobility within the world of production is confronted by rigid educational systems often incapable of coming to terms with the new place of knowledge in production within and between countries. The number of researchers and national commissions reporting upon these matters is a revealing indicator of economic progress.

Electronics, computer and robot technology, and bio-technology are affecting educational needs. But are these technologies skilling or deskilling people? This still needs to be studied, but in general new technologies demand mastering relevant knowledge.

New technologies are related to and create new organisational patterns, chosen by or imposed on the working class: therefore, new educational activities have to be developed by the workers themselves in order to negotiate the introduction of these technologies in the production system. And if the transformation of the production system means a reduction of working hours, new educational activities also have to be envisaged to enrich the increased leisure time created free-time induced by new technology and automation.

The progressive automation of production requires a major transformation of education; education must be extended to every aspect of life because an important part of each individual's active life will need to be devoted to educational activities.[31] But the impact of the educational system upon employment and unemployment appears to be less than that of unemployment upon education.

The problems posed for education by the different kinds of mobility and by the need to create jobs are numerous. Among such problems are: the relation between general education and more specialised vocational preparation; the relation between and integration of job creation at the local level and that of the national and international economy; the protection and strengthening of industrial employment or the bold planning for and development of non-industrial employment, especially in the service sector.

The Spread of Technology and the Developing Countries

The internationalisation of production and the emergence of powerful multinational corporations are giving rise to new forms of foreign investment and trade. Joint ventures, international subcontracts and international industrial co-operation are some of the emerging forms of foreign investment[32] which are giving rise to new dependence and interdependence in terms of both technology and training. These trends necessitate the provision of relevant training activities for national participants from marginal countries: this is in contrast to the former nature of foreign involvement (in the sale of centre-country products and direct investments) which required little investment in training. We have also to take in consideration that trade and production are affected by the impact of new technologies or organisational structures, by the internationalisation of the tertiary sector (research, engineering, informatics, management consulting) and by the introduction of small and medium-size enterprises in the international economy.[33]

The debate between Emmanuel and Furtado concerning technology in developing countries is still very relevant.[34] What is more important: to accept foreign technology or to make every effort to develop one's own technology? Perhaps a more dialogical approach is needed in the search for an alternative to the debate between autarchy and technological dependence. Emmanuel is right when he says that given peoples have cultures that are linked to their technological development; as a result, it is useless to search for technological developments appropriate for given cultures. Furtado is right when he warns against the implications of easy technological transfers that are not genuinely transfers of knowledge and mastery of these technologies.

There are many contradictory tendencies in the struggle against colonisation and other forms of domination. On the one hand, a new colonialism is developing, but, by contrast, many liberation movements are achieving concrete results with respect to national independence, women's liberation, minority rights, etc. Dominant new technology may be seen as an emerging form of colonialism, to which people from Third World countries may respond in the same way as they did to the introduction of education by the colonial powers. In Africa, for instance, some of those who were allowed to send their children to schools established by the colonial power either refused to send them or kept them in traditional education until they were 10-12 years old in order to ensure that they developed their own cultural identity. Only then did they allow their children to attend the colonists' schools. Similarly, people cannot ignore the dominant technological culture, but when they use it they msut ensure that they retain their own cultural identity and use those imported elements necessary for their own development.

Who has to pay for the importation of education and training? We are now witness to contradictory phenomena: there are limited 'gifts' such as aid to assist in the spread of 'literacy' or concerned with aspects of non-formal education; there are also very expensive imports to develop vocational training and education in combination with influx of technological products, higher education, and business consultancies. Another special 'educational import' is propaganda coming from wealthy and powerful countries: in this case there is no cost, but the consequences, as far as independence is concerned, are very high. New rules are needed concerning the financial aspect of inflow of educational ideas; developing countries are often obliged to spend too much for these educational imports, sometimes useless, sometimes very useful but still too expensive. Ignorance concerning education and training facilities contribute to the perpetuation of these unequal educational communications. China is one example of a country seeking to modify these educational imports to its own advantage. Such control is difficult, however, and dependent on the possession of some

Table 4.1: Impacts of the Spread of Technology[35]

	Positive	Negative
Short-term:	Sales of technology: processes, engineering, know-how, assistance Sales of equipment Opportunities for no-risk investment by simply providing technology	Loss of export markets Emergence of new competition (which may be disruptive) in domestic markets and third markets No job creation or loss of jobs in countries which have long-established competing industries

Medium and long-term	Opening of new markets with growing effective demand
	Dynamic reorganisation of long-established industries in the direction of advanced technologies, technological services, complex equipment, high-technology products
	Faster innovation
	  · improved processes
	  · improved product performance
	  · new products
	Availability of cheaper products
		Serious crisis in countries where structural rigidities and low technological potential inhibit adaptation to new competitive conditions

job creation

resources that can be used as a basis for bargaining.

The Spread of Technology and the Industrialised Countries

Industrialised countries are experiencing both the positive and negative impacts of the spread of technology. Moreover, they are faced with the continuous changes that result from this (see Table 4.1).

The Economic Crises of the 1980s

There are a number of potential crises in this period, including the exhaustion of technological progress, and the social limits of capitalism.[36] There are also crises for some countries while others are developing and problems for some given social groups while others are being supported. The representation of the relations between crisis and new technologies is often distorted. Economic and military competition[37] are responsible for technological development, therefore the role of the state and of industry are both relevant. Social classes can profit differently from technological progress in different ways, and even high-technology occupations[38] reflect occupational values related to social groups and classes. At the same time, technologies and techniques, as social products, are associated with the labour process, and the military imperative. Additionally, they are associated with gender differences — indeed partriarchal systems need to be studied.[39]

Notes

1. L.C. Pasinetti, *Structural Change and Economic Growth*, Cambridge, University Press, 1981
2. H. Makler, A. Martinelli and N. Smelser, *The New International Economy*, London, Sage, 1982
3. L.C. Pasinetti, Ibid
4. B. Bellon, C. Brochet and O. Pastre, Qui maîtrise la science et la technologie', Colloque 'Vers quel nouvel ordre mondial', *Atelier 13*, Paris, Université de Paris VIII, September 1983
5. Various authors, *International Migration Policies and Programmes, A World Survey*, New York, United Nations, 1982, pp. 22-6
6. OCDE, *Le défi du chômage*, Rapport aux Ministres du Travail, Paris, OECD, 1982, p. 119
7. M. Cavouriaris and K. Messamah, 'Migrations internationales et travailleurs migrants', Colloque 'Vers quel nouvel ordre mondial?', *Atelier 19*, Paris,

Université de Paris VIII, September 1983

8. C. Vimont, *L'avenir de l'emploi*, Paris, Economica, 1981, p. 184

9. Commissariat général du Plan, *Emploi éclaté, hommes dissociés*, Paris, La documentation française, 1982

10. C. Jedlicki, 'Les transferts internationaux de technologie comme forme de délocalisation de la production', *Revue Tiers-Monde*, T. XXIII, no. 91, July-September 1982

11. F. Novara, 'Note sui problemi di introduzione dei sistemi informativi automatizzati', *Problemi del socialismo*, no. 20, 1981, 43

12. C. Roche, 'Eléments pour un programme politique de réponse à la crise économique', *Les temps modernes*, April 1983

13. G. Payne and J. Payne, 'Occupational and Industrial Transition in Social Mobility', *The British Journal of Sociology*, vol. XXXIV, no. 1, March 1983, 72-89

14. P. Green, 'Prolegomena to a Democratic Theory of the Division of Labour', *The Philosophical Forum*, vol. XIV, no. 3-4, Spring-Summer 1983

15. Unesco, *Voix multiples, un seul monde*, Paris, Unesco, La documentation française/Nouvelles éditions africaines, 1980

16. E. Morin, *Pour sortir du XXème siècle*, Paris, Nathan, 1981, p. 358

17. C. Barrier-Lynn, Notes en marge de celle de Jean Lojkine *a propos d'automatisation a la japonaise'*, *Sociologie du travail*, no. 1, 1983, 63

18. L. Conti and C. Camera, *La technologie des origines à l'an 2.000*, Paris, Solars, 1981, pp. 334 et 336

19. A. Monclus Estella, 'Consideraciones sobre utopia, technica y educacion', *Universitas 2000*, vol. 6, no. 1, 1982 (Venezuela)

20. H.M. Levin and R.W. Rumberger, 'The Educational Implications of High Technology', National Institute of Education/Stanford University, February 1983, p. 5, mimeo

21. Various authors, *Technology, Growth, Employment*, Paris, La Documentation française, 1983

22. ILO, *World Labour Report*, Geneva, 1984, p. 3

23. Ibid.

24. OCDE, *la micro-électronique, la robotique et l'emploi*, Paris, OCDE, 1982, p. 75

25. F. Geze, 'Automatisation, productivité et emploi'; A. Fourçans et J-C. Yarondeau, 'Automatisation et emploi, mythes et réalités' in Adefi, *Les mutations technologiques*, Paris, Economica, 1981

26. M. Rustin, 'A strategy for Jobs', *New Left Review*, Jan.-Feb. 1983, 56-7

27. M. Warner, *The Impact of New Technology on Participative Institution and Employee*, Involvement, Dubrovnik, ISA, mimeo, 1983

28. W. Albeda, 'Reflections on the Future of Full Employment' (Part I), *Labour and Society*, vol. 7, no. 4, Oct.-Dec. 1982, 355-73; (Part II), *Labour and Society*, vol. 8, no. 1, Jan.-Mar. 1983, 57-71

29. Ires CGIL (ed.), *Obiettivo democrazia industriale*, Rome, ESI, 1980

30. A. Zimbalist (ed.), *Case Studies on the Labour Process*, New York, Monthly Review Press, 1979, p. 50

31. G. Friedericks and A. Schaff, *Microelectronics and Society, For Better and For Worse*, London, Pergamon Press, 1982

32. F. Momigliano and G. Balcet, 'Nuove forme d'investimento internazionale et teoria del coinvolgimento estero dell'impresa', *Economia e politica industriale*, Dec. 1982, 35-67

33. Ibid.

34. A. Emmanuel, *Technologie appropriée ou technologie sous-développée*, Paris, PUF, 1981

35. OCDE, *North-South Technology Transfer, The Adjustments Ahead*, Paris, OCDE, 1981, p. 53

36. F. Chesnais, 'Enjeux de la nouvelle technologie' Amérique latine, *Cetral*, Jan.-Mar. 1983

37. R. Kaplinsky, *Automation, the Technology and the Society*, London, Longman, 1984, pp. 22-3

38. V. Tomovic, *High Technological Occupations – Their status and Intra-occupational Ideologies*, Dubrovnik, ISA, 1983, mimeo

39. R. Kaplinsky, Ibid

5 LIVING WITHOUT WAGES

Employment and unemployment have to be seen within the current international division of labour, the segmentation of the labour market, the rapid pace of technological change within agriculture, industry, the service sectors and the fourth sector of research and development. At the same time, the problem of employment and unemployment has to be considered not only in economic terms but also in cultural, social and political terms. These different dimensions of work have implications for education, even if educators often do not seem to understand this.

In this perspective, some new educational approaches such as: interdisciplinarity, closer interrelationships between formal and non-formal education, use of teachers who are not educators, better coordination between general and vocational education, productive experience in education and educational experience in production — all can have a significant meaning. In fact, education has and will have to cope with a changing reality concerning social and productive life.

Unemployment is more and more considered as a permanent aspect of the current labour market. How can we react to this way of thinking? We have to recognise that unemployment is becoming a reality in most contemporary societies. But at the same time, we can work to reverse the situation through a new approach to work. Why do we not consider work as a right just as we consider health, education, housing? The statutory right to work is intended to transfer the resources of the state from maintaining citizens out of work, to maintaining them (the population of working age, that is) in work.[1]

Indeed, the implementation of the right to work means a full use of human resources in contemporary society. An active policy for jobs also means active policies concerning new jobs for educational and cultural activities, the conversion of military capital-intensive activities into labour-intensive activities, the improvement rather than just the protection of the environment, and the struggle against alienating work.

The unemployment of the 1980s is very often seen as a repetition of the unemployment situation of the 1930s. But, for example, in the 1930s 'the workers' conditions were not so high. They were near to subsistence level when they were working and below when not'.[2] In 1981 'Even the lowest income level was well above subsistence. However, it is far more psychologically difficult to bear unemployment than materially'.[3] In addition, while in the 1930s 'People lived just around the corner from their place of work',[4] in 1981 'the working class lived further and further away from their place of work'.[5] In the 1930s 'There existed a great sense of solidarity and "camaraderie" amongst the unemployed',[6] in 1981 'each unemployed person was either for him or herself'.[7] In the 1930s 'skilled workers were often amongst the first to be called back',[8] in 1981 'there were an increasing number of old/older people, 40+, both shop floor and white-collar workers, whose skills were completely useless'.[9]

Even in developed market economies significant sections of the population are suffering because of widespread unemployment (see Table 5.1).

Table 5.1: Selected Developed Market Economies: Unemployment Rates[a] 1976-84 (Percentage of Civilian Labour Force)[10]

Country or country group	1976-80	1981	1982	1983[a]	1984[b]
Major developed market economies	5.3	6.5	7.9	8.0	7.9
Canada	7.7	7.6	11.0	11.9	10.7
France	5.3	7.3	8.0	8.2	9.2
Germany, Federal Republic of	3.4	4.8	6.9	8.5	9.2
Italy	7.1	8.5	9.1	10.0	10.3
Japan	2.1	2.2	2.4	2.7	2.6
United Kingdom	6.4	10.6	11.0	11.5	11.6
United States	5.2	7.5	9.7	9.6	7.7
Other economies					
Belgium	8.2	10.7	12.6	14.5	15.3
Denmark	5.7	8.3	9.7	10.7	11.8
Ireland	8.5	10.2	11.7	14.6	16.6
Netherlands	4.3	7.1	12.7	15.6	17.6

Source: Department of International Economic and Social Affairs of the United Nations Secretariat, based in the case of the major countries on Organisation for Economic Co-operation and Development, *OECD Economic Outlook* and other official national sources, and in the case of other economies on Commission of the European Communites, *Annual Economic Report 1983-1984*.
Notes: a. Preliminary estimates.
b. Forecasts.

In the case of countries with planned economies, the problems of unemployment are less overt; in these countries there is a discrepancy between the qualifications obtained by school children and students and the nature of work awaiting them. There is some unemployment, but one mainly speaks of unskilled, poorly paid work, and few prospects for some categories of workers.

In developing countries urban unemployment is associated with a widespread underunemployment both in the rural and urban areas.

We have to avoid any generalisation concerning the conditions of young and adult workers who are without wages, for we do have: (a) young people and adults with work and without regular wages who are active in the non-formal sector of production; (b) young people and adults without wages and without work but with training and unemployment benefits; (c) young people and adults without wages, work, training and unemployment benefits.

The conditions among young people also vary considerably because there are young people with family support and young people without such support. It is clear that these different conditions also have consequences for their educational needs and demands.

Demographic trends and sex also have to be taken into consideration as far as unemployment is concerned. Increasingly, women try to be part of the active labour market. As far as young people and adults are concerned, different demographic trends will lead to different situations. As an example: today the industrialised countries are facing difficulties in providing youth with work: tomorrow they will likely be faced with the problem of maintaining adults in work because of the increasing age of their population and their decreasing adaptability to changing conditions of production.

Migration trends are also relevant for those countries that in the past sent their workers abroad. In some cases migration will be reduced, and some workers and their families will return home because of increasing automation and unemployment within the industrialised countries.

Unemployed people often create their own leisure and their own culture, to which the establishment reacts in two ways: either ignoring this culture or reacting defensively against new behaviours and models. The tramp is preferred to the existentialist for

the tramp becomes the inverted mirror image of the ideal middle class life. The middle classes see in the existentialist the reality of those impulses which generate their own fantasies and that, by contrast, in themselves these impulses are velleitary[11]

As far as unemployed young people are concerned, subcultures are developing which reflect their feelings about the difficulties they have in entering the social and productive systems. The *motards, svartingas*, skinheads, punks, teds, bikers, etc.[12] reflect different ways of life, very progressive or very racist, most of which are based on a rejection of an adult world they do not see any hope of entering. There is not the general youth culture that there was in the 1960s; now there are different subcultures which reflect the different experiences of those young people who do obtain employment and those who are excluded from employment for years – or even forever.

Young people are disturbed by the contradictions between the open educational ideologies (education for all) and the restricted educational practices in the societies of East and West, North and South. Open educational ideologies contrast with strong social structures that are developing selective educational practices. Therefore, the educational and cultural experiences sought for by young people are often very far removed from the provisions offered by formal institutions. Good examples include the 'flying universities' of Eastern Europe and the anti-nuclear youth movements of Western Europe and USA. Unfortunately, these different groups have difficulties in communicating among themselves. In addition, the possible contributions of comparative education and comparative cultural development are often blocked as they are controlled by the most conservative institutions of the countries concerned, full of rhetoric but with no concern for the emerging educational and cultural trends.

The following examples reflect the collective will which has in some instances reacted positively and creatively to the conditions of unemployment and the motivation to create new patterns of work:

(1) In Mondragon, the headquarters of the Basque co-operative movement is composed of 127 federated co-operatives. Among them there are free-service co-operative: one is controlled and owned by women; another is a popular workers' bank; another is concerned with social security and medical service; another is a modern centre of research and development; and the fifth is a league of culture and education, a grouping of 30 educational co-operatives. The workers participate in decisions about production, organisation and general policy. In the educational activities, students are trained in preparation for future active participation, job sharing, rotation of tasks, involvement in the planning of tasks and plant operation.[13]

(2) Marinaleda is an Andalusian village with a very high percentage of unemployed people. To try to overcome this dramatic situation, the

mayor and the municipality took strong action in two directions: (i) a hunger strike was started to force regional and national authorities to recognise the problem; (ii) voluntary work in the commune was developed to build up the educational, cultural and social services badly needed by the people. In a few years this village created educational and cultural centres; transformed a poor physical environment into a very rich one as far as roads and trees were concerned; began developing co-operatives and forced the authorities into supportive action.[14]

(3) How do men and women react when forced to give up their occupations and receive unemployment benefits? A study was undertaken in Turin among unemployed workers receiving unemployment benefits to answer this question.[15] As far as the use of time was concerned, significant differences emerged between men and women:

| | Percentage of time spent | |
Activity	Men	Women
Domestic	5.5	55.9
Unions, party	25.3	11.8
Sports, hobbies, culture	18.7	17.6
Social life	14.3	14.7
Work	5.5	0
Inertia	30.8	0

The study also showed that in periods of unemployment the family relationships improved for 26.7 per cent of men and 35.3 per cent of women, and worsened for 24.4 per cent of men and 8 per cent of women. It was also much easier for women to find work and participate in vocational training and thereby maintain contact with colleagues.

(4) The informal sector of production is already the most important one in developing countries, but it is also becoming important in industrial societies. In a study on the informal sector of production in Colombo (Sri Lanka)[16] the relevance of this sector was underlined and some suggestions were made on giving support to this sector, which involved the majority of the urban population.

Three types of policies were proposed for different aspects of the informal sector: (a) some parts of the informal sector were left alone to adjust by themselves and these parts were the most marginal, their strength being their marginality; (b) for other sectors (tailoring, shoe-manufacturing, etc.) public support was envisaged to enable these activities to survive the strong competition with the industrial sector; (c) for some important parts of the urban economy such as vegetables, trade and transport, light-engineering policies were advocated to improve efficiency and productivity, to generate employment, and to introduce modern technology in the informal sector.[17]

(5) Legislation for temporary jobs is evolving in many industrial countries, and legislation from the 1950s and 1960s is being revised. One example for organising temporary jobs is that of the French agency Etic (temporary jobs through co-operatives). To avoid abuse, this agency distributes 70 per cent of its profits among co-operative workers and has a limited scale of salaries. The anticipated results for these workers' co-operatives are reduced employment, better qualifications and new social integration: the conditions are the acceptance of the mobility and the mastering of skills by the workers, and activities with a fixed-term contract.

(6) Solomon Mahlangu Freedom College (SOMAFCO) of the African National Congress (ANC) is a dramatic example of an attempt to link closely productive work and education. Its objective is to provide an alternative education to that of the racist regime of South Africa through the elimination of the gap between manual and mental labour.[18]

> The project should provide for training, education and employment and should gradually introduce and extend collective ownership and cooperative practices amongst its members — not only in respect of production for income, but also in respect of mutual support in directly satisfying a whole range of needs for themselves and their families, e.g. producing most of the food they eat and building their homes. It is necessary that participants make small but regular contributions in labour, kind or cash towards capital formation. Full participation in the direct control of their affairs would be an essential feature and the programme should extend far beyond purely economic activities, to include political, cultural, recreational, social and educational activities as well.[19]

(7) Seasonal work with regular or irregular wages occurs in the agriculture sector. In an enquiry that was made in an English village in Suffolk,[20] the most valued aspects of their jobs given by agricultural workers were the following in descending order of interest:

Satisfaction from seeing crops and
    animals grow
Outdoors

Variety
Autonomy
Money
Working with Machinery

These different evaluations indicate that the informal sector of production is creating job opportunities for workers without regular wages. With respect to the debate concerning the relevance of the informal sector of production to the solution of the problem of unemployment, it is suggested that the development of enterprises concerned with the social environment is still the main answer to the creation and maintenance of jobs. At the same time, it is also possible that a growing number of the newer occupations in computer software, telecommunications, retailing, management consulting will stimulate the creation of self-employment.[21]

The new relevance of production and knowledge, and their diffusion also affects possibilities for self-employment; for knowledge, research and training are becoming some of the most important productive activities. Legal and regulatory frameworks need to be developed to avoid exploitation in the non-formal sector and in self-employment. Are new technologies creating jobs or reducing them? Three million new jobs will be created in Italy within ten years, the majority of which are closely linked to new technologies: computers (450,000), administration (300,000), new agricultural technologies (300,000), management, maintenance and use of industrial robots (200,000), energy techniques (200,000), production and use of special materials (200,000).[22]

New technologies necessitate educational systems that are able to cope with new educational demands. Currently, our educational systems often produce young people who are handicapped by inadequate educational qualifications. This raises problems, as 'educationally handicapped people' have difficulties in integrating themselves with the existing productive system, and are becoming more familiar with new technologies.[23]

Education for Unemployment and Education for the Creation of New Jobs

Sometimes, educational institutions and educators do not seem to be working toward the creation of jobs because of ignorance, narrow cultural perspectives and little contact with the world of work. Educators have to become directly involved in the world of work if they want to be of relevance to the needs of youth and adults seeking jobs and fighting for survival. Because of the limited nature of their experience, they have difficulties in training young and adult people for the rapidly changing world of work.

National policies in the field of work and education are poorly co-ordinated in the formal and non-formal sectors of production. Communication between the productive and educational systems is difficult. A very limited amount of time and space is devoted to educational purposes within both systems.

New values concerning work, leisure and employment are developing, and working time and non-working time have new meanings, but little attention is paid by policy-makers and educators to these new values. Young people are asking for active job policies, in anticipation of the emerging needs of modern society concerning educational, cultural and social development. In cases where new job creation is taking place spontaneously, governments need to support these initiatives; in other cases it is up to governments to take the initiative. Better coordination between the formal and non-formal sectors of production will aid this effort at job creation.

Serious efforts are needed on the part of the different structures of the formal sector of production, unions and governmental agencies to bridge the gap between workers belonging to the formal and non-formal sectors of production. The present sharp separation between these two categories of workers will have negative consequences to the social system, and will create, in a short period of time, two different categories of citizens.

Education has an important role in this respect. Unfortunately, the tendency is to create special separate programmes for unemployed people which allow no contact with other employed people. Education can help in dismantling the barriers between employment and unemployment and in opposing the tendency to develop the capacities of a minority to the neglect of the majority. Although this practice is justified on the basis of efficiency 'the belief that we can possibly be maximising overall social intelligence and thus overall social utility, in this way, is better classified as a bizarre superstition.'[24] It is only through innovative and creative policies that mounting 'apathy, frustration, frozen anxiety and violence and the feeling of failure' can be combated.[25] Loneliness and an apparently hopeless future can lead young people to violence towards the self through suicide, drugs and/or alcohol and to rebellion against the outside world. The creation of jobs, the right to work and overcoming alienating work should be the main targets of every society seeking to give meaning to the concept of democracy.

But the global crisis does not have to discourage people, as the following quotation shows:

All four of us [Amin − Middle East, Arrighi − Europe, Gunder Frank − Latin America, Wallerstein − North America] however, continue to believe that human social action to transform the world is still possible, desirable, and urgent. All believe the world is indeed in a long-term structural 'crisis', and that intelligent reflection is a priority to which we must all give allegiance.[26]

Notes

1. M. Rustin, 'A Statutory Right to Work', *New Left Review*, no. 137, Jan.-Feb. 1983, 56
2. R. Hauser, *A New Beginning for the Unemployed*, London, The Institute of Social Research, 1981
3. Ibid.
4. Ibid.
5. Ibid.
6. Ibid.
7. Ibid.
8. Ibid.
9. Ibid.
10. United Nations, *World Economic Survey 1984*, New York, 1984
11. P. Crisp, 'The Existentialist and the Tramp', *The Crane Bag*, 1978, p. 144
12. 'Youth Tribes', *Time*, October 1983
13. C. Ornelas, 'The Producer Cooperatives of Mondragon and the Combination of Study with Productive Labour', *Work With Production*, December 1981
14. J.M. Sancez Gordillo, *Marinaleda, Andaluces, Levantaos,* Granada, Alyibe, 1980
15. Isfol-Regione Piemonte *Caratteristiche e comportamenti degli operai Fiat in mobilità*, Rome, Isfol, 1983
16. Marga Institute, *The Informal Sector in Colombo City* (Sri Lanka), Colombo, Marga Institute, 1979
17. Ibid.
18. A. Mrubatha, 'Education and Production at SOMAFCO', *FEB Newsletter* (The Foundation for Education with Production), no. 11, March 1984, 8
19. P. Van Rensburg, *Looking Forward from Serowe*, Gaborone (Botswana), The Foundation for Education with Production, 1984
20. H. Newby, *The Deferential Worker*, London, Penguin, 1977
21. R. Russell, 'Employee Ownership in the Services', Mimeo, 1983
22. V. Colombo 'Uno nessuno tre millioni', in 'Viaggio al Centro del Lavoro', *L'Unita*, 1 May 1984
23. A. Walker, *Unqualified and Underemployed Handicapped Young People*

and the Labour Market, London, National Children's Bureau, 1982, p. 44

24. P. Green, 'Prolegomena to a Democratic Theory of the Division of Labour', *The Philosophical Forum*, no. 3-4 1983, 290

25. R. Hauser, *A New Beginning*

26. J. Amin, G. Arrighi, A. Gunder Frank and I. Wallerstein, *Dynamics of Global Crisis*, New York, Monthly Review Press, 1982

6 YOUTH AND ADULT WORKERS' EDUCATION

The Transformation of the Productive and Social Systems and Their Relevance for Education

The entire educational process needs to be reviewed, including youth and adult worker education. We often have a narrow understanding of the theory and practice of worker education and this perhaps left over from a period when worker education was identified solely with the education of the employed workers of industrial societies.

Today we have broadened the concept of worker, and we include in this term the totality of youth and adults working in the primary, secondary, tertiary, quaternary (research and development) sectors of production. Worker education includes initial and further training, formal and non-formal education, union training, general education and education for leisure.

There are many signs that people are fighting not only to obtain education but also to participate in its planning. Youth, parents and workers are coming to understand the relevance not only of education but also of the goals and the quality of this or that type. Participation is not only a hope, but it is realised practice as a result of many struggles. People are more and more aware of the relevant link between different sectors and periods of education, and they are dissatisfied when they are confined to only one of them.

Radical changes in the productive system have and will have more and more direct and indirect consequences for education: shifts from traditional to modern agriculture, and from agriculture towards industry and then towards the tertiary and quaternary sectors of production. All these changes may mean a broader initial general education for everybody, and not only for a limited elite. Unfortunately, these radical transformations in the productive system are not always known in the world of education, especially in some countries where economic decisions are often taken without the diffusion of information to the larger society.

The implications of worker mobility for education is also another aspect that has to be taken into consideration; geographic mobility (migrants, refugees, international experts, etc.) implies that there are new educational needs to cope not only with new technologies but also with new cultural environments.

The continuing technological and scientific revolution was often seen as good in itself. This is true if workers are able to master the processes of change and to influence its outcome. Without struggle and negotiation the working class and society in general can be split into two sectors: one which benefits largely from this scientific and technological revolution, and another which suffers from it (unemployment, underemployment, compulsory early retirement, social marginalisation, etc.). The automation and computerisation of society lead to unemployment for some people and new jobs for others. It is important to find means of eliminating the cleavage between people that partially results from their different levels of initial and further education and training.

We have to get rid of the traditional clearly demarcated work-leisure dichotomy of the industrial world. Working and non-working time are coming to have a new meaning and a new relationship one to the other. The cultural and educational dimensions of work are becoming more relevant and even central; at the same time, non-working time, free or imposed, is growing for a great number of people. If formal education has done little for the needs of working time, it has done even less for those of non-working time (unemployment, leisure, family time, non-formal education).

A great variety of new development needs and goals[1] is emerging: peace, people participation and self-management, survival skills, self-actualisation, individual and collective human rights, cultural identity, and intra-and inter-personal relationships. These goals are considered important by people and in our societies and a great deal of time is invested in their achievement. But formal education has done very little to prepare people to struggle for these goals. Educational institutions often consider that these goals are purely moral or philosophical declarations, but people want to achieve them not merely talk about them. The introduction into the educational system of activities leading to these goals means a full reshaping of educational programmes: worker education should be strongly involved in this educational rethinking.

The new relevance of knowledge and the production of knowledge require new educational policies and activities. The manufacture of knowledge is becoming one of the most dynamic productive activities. Countries which are able to develop this special kind of production are diverting large resources from economic production into institutions for initial and further training since it is recognised that these are vital to the production of knowledge.

Education is also becoming a part of production time. In workers' career in several sectors of manufacture, educational time has become an integrated part of the workers' lives. The spreading of knowledge and training between countries is also developing rapidly because of the development of communication techniques, the migration of peoples and the internationalisation of economies. The spreading of knowledge and education implies new contents of an intercultural nature in the educational process.

Education is affected by the widespread development of communication and information,[2] but until now this evidence did not imply a positive and dialectic relationship between education and communication. On one side education rejects this relationship, on the other side it is becoming its prisoner. And worker education does not escape this dichotomy. Most of the formal and non-formal worker education is done indirectly through the media, but the traditional workers education institutions have no impact on media education.

The main struggles of the workers for education are being fought or have to be fought within the productive system.[3] First, they have to fight to bring the younger generation into productive work by increasing solidarity with youth so as to prevent the creation of groups of youngsters lacking hope and isolated from the world of work. Secondly, the internationalisation of the labour market has to alert workers to the danger of the sometimes open and sometimes hidden racism which divides workers and creates conflict between them. Thirdly, a new cultural and educational awareness has to be developed which takes into account the great variety of cultural contributions coming from workers all over the world, with no limitation as to country, sex, race, age, etc.

Through these cultural and educational struggles, workers can contribute to new educational policies and can enlarge their own educational perspectives. Unfortunately, a considerable provincialism characterises the great majority of educational systems, and the self-perpetuation of these systems is often stronger than the desire to be open to new cultural and educational influences. Open, flexible and dynamic educational systems are to the benefit of the workers who are today often rejected by the rigid barriers and access of self-perpetuating educational systems.

New working class movements are often little known; knowledge of the history of the working class of industrial countries is increasing, but only a restricted amount of information is circulating on the plight of workers who are struggling now in the plantations, in the shanty towns, and in the ports of the so-called peripheral countries. Although their conditions are not much different from those of the western working class of the nineteenth or even eighteenth centuries, few show an interest in overthrowing exploitation. Long working hours, child labour, poor health conditions, inadequate housing are all condoned by silence. It is indeed a wide field for research and action in international education, but who is concerned? In dealing with developing countries, international federations of unions are often concerned only with their own members, who represent only a small minority of the working class of these countries, and/or with spreading their ideologies. The marginality of the economies of these developing countries make it difficult for local workers to organise themselves and develop negotiating power. As far as educational and adult education associations are concerned, their activities are still limited to traditional literacy programmes or to very narrow vocational-training activities.

New illiteracy, computer illiteracy, functional illiteracy: these new concepts are circulating, and workers seem to be again in a condition of dependency and marginality. New skills are needed, but the lack of mastery of these skills does not mean that the workers are incapable of participating fully in political, social and cultural life. It is only through participation that workers will achieve the right to be informed, to take part in, and not be merely passive spectators of cultural activities. It is only through such participation that they will achieve the right to work. Hence, trade union, co-operative and consumer education has to be forward looking.

Trade union education should not simply be the education of trade union officers; general education, self-management aid, new technological literacy for all workers (unemployed and migrant workers included) have to be included in union education. This can occur when a dialectic relationship between more formal institutional education and trade union education is established — and this can be profitable for both union and institutional education. But union education is a mirror of the level of union democracy, and the most interesting educational experiences are a result of a wide popular participation in union life and of an internationalism that is neither manipulated nor one sided.

Neither should co-operative education be limited to the officers of the co-operatives.[4] The need for co-operation is emerging in agriculture, in industry and in the broad services sector. Youth job creation is often connected with co-operatives, and co-operatives can work for the survival of small and medium-size farms and factories. But, as far as continuing education is concerned, co-operative education is mostly absent in formal initial education, and is limited to the existing co-operative movements. Advanced self-management in modern society requires co-operative experiences within educational, productive, social, administrative and cultural systems. Self-management is necessary to cope with the uncertainties of a long period of transition, during which time there is a need to make shared collective decisions concerning pro-duction, education, social policy and a need for, but lack of infor-mation, upon which the decision-making process may be based.

Consumer education often reflects a defensive attitude of consumer associations. Consumers can play an important role in the re-shaping of production, therefore consumer education must be linked with initial and further training. In such education aesthetics are as relevant as economics, mathematics and accounting. The consumer demand from wealthy countries has important consequences for the life of millions of people in the marginal countries, and a purely defensive attitude on the part of consumers means merely the protection of the most protected.

A new international order of education is both a consequence of and a powerful instrument for the maintenance of a new world economic order. Positive educational discrimination – which must be a feature of this new international order – within and among countries – means taking in account the disparity of educational facilities and opportuni-ties, and finding ways and means to overcome it. Financial wealth and economic superiority neither imply the right to cultural leadership, nor does it produce better quality education in the more privileged groups and countries; intercultural and intereducational co-operation and exchange on a basis of equality are therefore a pre-condition for meaningful positive educational discrimination. Workers' education can be either an instrument for liberation or for submission to paterna-listic control. Workers' education can reinforce authoritarian education or it can associate the peoples' individual and collective daily educa-tional needs with specific technological and scientific societal goals.

Worker education for today and tomorrow can make use of its own traditions, but it must not become the prisoner of these traditions. Learning from past experience and the encouragement of new ideas are not contradictory. The rich inheritance of the working class experience from all over the world can lead to creative cultural identity but also to meaningless rhetoric. The conditions of workers are changing, new differences are arising, others are disappearing. Action, struggle, empathy, and not the pedagogical and ideological rhetoric of the past, are the foundations of new unity among workers within and among

countries. Creative education can be disturbing, but history proves that
it is a worthwhile risk.

Educational Spaces, Times, Methods and Techniques Adapted to Adult Learning

New educational policies and practices imply new educators and new
educational time, space, content, methods and media, – all these
of which are interconnected. The learning process is extending beyond
schooling, vocational training and third age education; educational time
is increasing within working and non-working time and tends to be
more flexible. Educational space becomes a continuum in the life of
children, youth and adults. Formal educational institutions cope only
with part of the demand: individual and collective self-education is to
be found in daily life in the most unexpected places even if there are
no bridges, or very limited ones, between this learning and more formal
education. The media are providing persuasive education daily and it is
there where popular participation is most noticeably absent. New
learning experiences are appearing and developing through these different experiences and highlighting the gap between them and the educational institutions. New methods have different origins: they come
either from very sophisticated and costly experiments (television, computers, etc.) or from a more spontaneous self-education through
cultural, leisure and working activities. New educators are appearing,
mainly from the world of work and leisure; efforts are made by educational institutions to use or to 'assimilate' them, but they (artists,
scientists, technologists, researchers) are often able to escape these
constricting tendencies, and creative education continues to develop
itself.

Education, as a lifetime learning process, requires not only more
educational time and space but also new methodologies, facilities and
techniques that are able to cope with the multiple processes of
knowing, valuing and doing. Education for all and education by all
imply an educational process in which research, creation, production,
teaching and learning are interlinked, and in which, in some way, all
participants are also involved in the production of educational hard
and software.

Local, national and international contexts are changing; these
changes provoke ruptures, changes and new directions in the social,
political, economic and cultural spheres. Traditional patterns of action

often lose their effectiveness and sometimes even their meaning. Popular participation for social transformation to respond to emerging needs which arise as a result of wide-ranging changes, arises only from the understanding that there is a need to act, and that action can be effective.

In order for educational systems to assist in community action, new structures and methodologies are needed. The transformation of educational systems requires the dissolution of the space/time/age divisions in education. The depth and quality of popular participation in the running of society will determine whether such charges result in greater articulation between the different educational systems: formal and non-formal, initial and continuing, vocational and general, institutional or self-instruction.

Popular responses to changing patterns in the productive process, (internationalisation, technological developments, labour-market segmentation), in family life (decreasing stability and tendencies towards both nuclear and extended family structures in response to wider socio-economic trends, fertility and mortality patterns), in leisure (universalisation of ideas and practices of leisure activities, more time, expansion of the role of the media in leisure time) are stimulating the development of specific methodologies to satisfy new learning needs. New educators are emerging in response to new educational demands and new educational objectives; their training is mainly in-service and often lacks an understanding of the culture of people with whom they will work.

International encounters have a cultural dimension, but few efforts are made to understand the cultural references of other people. Because of the failure to take into account these different cultural realities, differencies in motivation among the participants are created, and areas of disagreement and conflict, are glossed over when resolution is possible.

Education for understanding, for communication, for survival and for participation in decision-making necessitate methods and techniques founded on participatory research, respect of individual and collective motivation, creativity, a spirit encouraging enquiry, collaborative work, individual and collective self-education, formative evaluation and self-management.

The recognition of popular cultures is a necessary condition for popular participation; ignoring cultural content in education programmes limits the true value of the education. Popular culture, aspirations, motivations, goals are the necessary foundations of educational programmes and modules if they are to be successful both within and outside the institution.

The specific learning methods (case study, programmed instruction, individualised instruction, computer-assisted instruction, group work, formative evaluation, simulation games, self-education) are useful for formal and non-formal education; they can be effective if they are related to concrete situations and active practice.

Self-instruction, the oldest form of education known to man, is evolving rapidly. Advances in communication systems applied to the educational field, the often uncontrollable problems of urbanisation, the increasing cost of transportation, the weak links between training structures and professional activity, migration between town and country and from one country to another, the increase in non-working time (leisure, unemployment, underemployment, retirement) are all encouraging the development of new forms of self-instruction that are more flexible and more effective in terms of time and cost.

In the training of educators, educational methodology and techno-logy are acquired through direct experience and some formalised teach-ing; the equilibrium between the two is sometimes difficult to achieve because of excessive claims for spontaneous teaching, or conformism in the institutional training of educators. Participation by future edu-cators in decision-making processes and activities is of paramount importance. Co-operation, self-management, community work, the practice of educational democracy, participatory research, in-service training, cultural activities are therefore very valuable experiences in the training of professional and voluntary educators because they familiarise future educators with the actual needs, problems and moti-vations of people.

Control over the choice and development of methods and tech-niques is demanded by the taught and not only by the professional teachers. People need to master learning processes if they are to play an active part in the daily reality of living, producing, creating, loving and amusing themselves, and so that they can fight against different forms of alienation. Therefore, participatory methodologies and techniques and financial resources should be made available to everybody; often these methodologies and technologies are discovered and created by the people themselves, and where this happens educational institutions have to both recognise and support them.

Educational activities and the training of educators require the con-tribution of qualified people in the different fields of science, techno-logy, arts, economy, crafts, agriculture, industry, poetry, management

and human development, music and social sciences. The mere transmission of educational technology and methodology is empty and even
can be manipulative if it is not associated with substantial input;[5]
this interdisciplinary work is again a form of participation by the
ordinary people possessing widely differing skills.

Education in international relations needs special forms of participatory methods enabling marginal countries and neglected social
groups not only to have access to education but also to determine their
own educational programmes. All projects should keep in perspective
the wider development needs of the country as a whole while concen-
trating on the needs of specific communities and subgroups. Positive
discrimination can be used to improve the situation of those who are
weaker in socio-economic terms.

The progressive internationalisation of education and culture stimulates, or should stimulate, research in and understanding of different
cultures. Intercultural educational activities are also developing within
productive, social, community and family groups. The failure of such
programmes is often related to the lack of real interest in, concern and
understanding of other cultures, national, foreign and migrant. International educational activities, networks, associations, organisations will
benefit by acquiring relevant cultural contributions from various
countries and peoples.

Notes

1. I. Bialecki and J. Sikorska, 'In the Sphere of Human Needs and Aspirations',
Sisyphus Sociological Studies, vol. III, *Crises and Conflicts — The Case of Poland
1980-81*, pp. 188-205
2. A. Toffler, *The Third Wave*, New York, Bantam Books and William Morrow,
1981
3. K. Mackie, 'The Significance of the Work-place for Adult Education', *International Journal of Lifelong Education*, vol. 2, no. 2, 174-88
4. J. Albaraccin Gomez, 'Necesidades en materia de formación cooperativa en
Bolivia', *Fencomin*, 1984, La Paz, mimeo, 3 pp
5. J.K. Nyerere, 'The Intellectual Needs Society', *Man and Development*,
Nairobi, London, New York, Oxford University Press, 1974

PART THREE: THE SEARCH FOR AND THE
IMPORTANCE OF CULTURE

7 CULTURE IN THE CITY, RURAL ENVIRONMENT AND COMMUNITY DEVELOPMENT

Culture in the City

The proportion of population living in urban areas (see Table 7.1) is growing, and this growth concerns all regions of the world. New cultural values, ways of life and needs are emerging in the urban setting.

Training and self-education in preparation for and occasional mastery of the foreseeable and often uncertain future is perhaps one of the requisites of contemporary urban, and specifically city, life. One dimension of this training and self-education is based upon popular participation in the variety of cultural experiences associated with work, leisure, social, emotional and community life.

One of the most striking elements of modern society is the great disregard and waste of human creative resources, intellectual and physical. Cultural activity directed to the development of a sense of self, is one aspect of cultural action which requires greater consideration.

As a matter of fact, we speak of protection of the cultural heritage, but in many cases we remain indifferent to the gradual retrogressive effect of stagnant cultures on men and women whose traditional skills and abilities tend to decline for lack of both utilisation and new challenges. The young, who on leaving school often fail to find permanent work, begin to question their own initial training and are consequently discouraged from pursuing further learning. Workers, displaced from the productive process because of technological advances or because of a decline in their productive energies, within a few years experience both the atrophy of their professional skills, and the breakdown of personal and social relationships, through frustration.

Action, research, and cultural development in a broad sense, can all contribute a solution to one of the most vital problems of our contemporary society — the creation of jobs. The lack of development in the field of research and failure to encourage the development of culture, particularly for developing countries, results in dependence on foreign imports and retards the development of local research capacity. In addition, it involves the draining away of substantial funds in royalties for the utilisation of foreign patents, with the effective loss of

Table 7.1: Percentage of the Population Living in Urban Areas: World, More Developed and Less Developed Regions, and Major Areas, 1950-2000

Area	1950	1960	1970	1975	1980	1985	1990	1995	2000
World	29.4	33.6	37.0	38.3	39.9	41.6	43.6	45.8	48.2
More developed regions	53.6	60.3	66.4	68.7	70.6	73.4	74.2	76.0	77.7
Less developed regions	17.4	21.4	25.3	27.1	29.4	31.8	34.4	17.3	40.4
Africa	14.8	18.4	22.9	25.6	28.7	32.1	35.5	38.9	42.2
Latin America	41.1	49.3	57.4	61.5	65.4	69.0	72.1	74.7	76.0
Northern America	63.9	69.9	73.8	73.9	73.8	74.3	75.2	76.4	78.0
East Asia	17.8	23.1	26.3	27.0	28.0	28.0	30.2	32.0	34.2
South Asia	16.1	18.3	21.2	23.2	25.4	27.7	30.4	33.5	36.8
Europe	55.9	60.5	66.2	68.6	71.1	73.7	75.4	77.2	78.9
Oceania	61.2	66.3	70.8	71.7	71.6	71.7	71.9	72.3	73.1
USSR	39.3	48.8	56.7	60.0	63.2	66.3	69.2	71.9	74.3

Source: Results of United Nations demographic estimates and projections as assessed in 1982.

future employment. The development of culture and research can also lead to the creation of extensive employment in the advanced sectors of production and, possibly, in arts and cultural infrastructures, which may be overlooked during periods of intensive economic development.

In a dynamic perspective the traditional boundaries between the cultures of the highly educated, the bourgeoisie, and the proletariat are becoming blurred, and new dialectic relations are emerging. The decade of the seventies saw the crisis both in purely proletarian culture and of the 'learned and bourgeois' culture of classical origin common to several Eastern and Western countries. Different and varied cultural, artistic, literary, scientific, technological, economic and political expressions will become manifest in the struggle between a living culture and a conformist culture; between the congealed culture of the establishment and the creative expression of cultural and social movements.

The first discovery which strikes those actively engaged in cultural action within the city is the limited knowledge that exists of needs and demands, the images of the cultures of the city-dwellers. This ignorance is reinforced by the frequent changes in the patterns of working life and social life of those in work and those without work. They are subject to migration, to the development of non-formal work, to increased unemployment, etc.[2] Hence the need for intensive research, especially in those parts of the city where there are new settlements.[3]

In this respect, the research carried out in Buenos Aires, Sao Paulo, Vitoria, is most interesting:[4] cultural activities in the outskirts of Vitoria and Sao Paulo (Brazil) and Buenos Aires (Argentina) are characterised by a separation of the consumers and the creators of cultural work, through a one-way communication in cultural activity, and through the formidable difficulties in transferring cultural experience to different social situations. Participation in community action stimulates the emergence of culturally critical groups, to more situations in which the leaders learn to act as mediators between the local communities and a global society, and this gives the people often subsisting in appalling conditions, the historic sense of struggle which underlines the fact that present situations are the result of the creative struggles of the past. Their participation, nevertheless, is quite passive, and only a minority are engaged in decision-making. As far as their collective needs are concerned, there exists a contradiction between the 'objective' needs of participation, creation, and recreation on the one hand, and on the other hand the 'subjective' needs, which include limited opportunities for research and information, training and strong tendencies of escapism. There exists a feeling that non-material needs are necessary, but the recognition of this factor does not always result in a coherent course of action.

If culture is to be accepted as an instrument of communication between different countries and civilisations, how do local and/or regional cultural developments check or promote greater cultural understanding? How much is the search for a cultural identity an instrument for a free or an inhibited creativity?

Cultural action in the city, which takes into account the special nature of local problems, can become an instrument for a better understanding of new problems, such as the relations between North-South, East-West; the rapport between national social systems and the international division of labour; the internationalisation of economies and particularly of financial markets; the great internal migrations on a continental and intercontinental scale; the spread of and the need to import technologies; the increasing number of refugees and exiles; the expansion of tourism at a global level, etc. These developments are transforming the environments in which people are living, and are often dramatically dangerous to peoples' ways of life.

How then do local and regional cultural developments hinder or enhance such communication? How much is the search for cultural identity an instrument of free or inhibited creativity?

Popular culture and mass cultures in the city are influenced by the above factors, but the promoters of cultural activities and researchers have an inflexible image of these cultures. They fail to understand that these factors have an impact on mutual relations between folk culture and mass culture. Culture also entails contributions to economic local and regional development in the national and international context; it is here that the folk culture finds itself at a loss, and where mass culture becomes an implement for domination. Scientific, economic, technological cultures too should become more self-critical in order to contribute to the enrichment of cultural life.

From cultural creation to cultural consumption: does this relation exist; to what extent is it dialectic and to what extent is it reciprocal?

A cultural policy which would contribute to and share in forms of cultural creation should be seen within two perspectives: the establishment of conditions which allow a maximum of direct participation in creative cultural work and the creation of the optimum condition for encouraging the creativity and independence of creative artists in their own spheres. Because artists can introduce a fresh outlook and raise new questions, they are not only significant for their creative cultural work, but equally for their contribution to the mass media and to the educational and community structures, and the world of work.

Cultural practices from this perspective need to be jointly formulated, so that new opportunities for cultural and creative activity are provided. In the 12th arrondisement of Paris, at Bercy, there was a project in which the planners invited the people to join with them in the transformation of the environment through the use of essential resources. The activities included: the replanning of cultural activities at Bercy in co-operation with architects; public workshops of the plastic arts; the development of different means of expression, that is, of posters, books, reproduction in copper-plate engraving silk-screen process, photocopies and other printing processes; organising individual and collective exhibitions.[5]

Folk culture and mass culture are present in the relations between contemporary social movements and the various social institutions of today. Folk culture and mass culture can contribute to the reinforcement, to the replication of the social system or to the promotion of democratisation and development. But folk culture is not always oriented towards evolution and creation; there are examples of folk culture inhibiting change. Folk and mass cultures which promote self-reliance rather than dependence in the social, economic and educational fields permit greater popular participation and control in all areas of life. The experience of the journal *Droit de Parole* of Quebec is an example of cultural action that brings together mass culture and folk culture. This journal has become an instrument of communication between groups of employees, and its aim is to provide a means for training those working for the improvement of working-class life in Quebec.

'Culture' is to be taken in its wider significance, where it is conceived not as a static end-product but more as a innovative and creative process. Community media must become the particular medium for the public expression of ideas and of existing lifestyles.[6]

The production or reproduction of social and vocational aspirations stimulates a conflict between the cultures of different classes, and they themselves are the result of these conflicts. In the city and in general in 'modern societies, the production of aspirations as a means and as a result of strong mobility of social-vocational and occupational status prevails.'[7] This conflict between cultures is magnified by the international dimension of change, economic, political, social, cultural.

The building of a city is also an expression of a desire to involve the inhabitants in the city's structure and its maintenance. Does communication between inhabitants and political leaders, urbanites, architects, administrators of leisure, educational and cultural structures, constitute a cultural activity in itself? Living in the city offers opportunity for the receipt and exchange of cultural experiences. Yet there is little research to ascertain the cultural motivations and interests, actual or only apparent, of the inhabitants — and these are also relevant cultural experiences. In the city, the crisis concerning values is perhaps more severe than in the rural area. It is the city which has developed such concepts as: 'welfare state', 'liberal democracy', etc. and they have become widely accepted concepts. The relevance of these values leads to crises and changes, in social relations, in production and in leisure. The crisis in values disturbs the inertia of folk cultures, and it is the starting point of many forms of mass culture.

Take the case of migrant workers' communities. The city can limit itself to making available to them only some of its cultural and educational services; or it can put at their disposal all the public facilities which can thus become centres for cultural creation and inter-communication with the indigenous populations of the various districts of this city.

The culture of the city also comprises the culture of migrant workers struggling for better conditions of life — not only for themselves but also for those others who still reside in their home countries. A group of African workers, engaged in a campaign in Paris against the construction of a dam in their own country which, undertaken without prior consultation with the African population, reflects features of urban culture which often go unnoticed.[8]

The specific nature of each cultural activity does not exclude some problems common to all such activities. The problems of the avant-garde, the cinema for example, are to be found in other aspects of cultural life.

The avant-garde cannot deny the present state of the cinema. They must bear with the existing situations in order to stir them up; for example, to work out a non-narrative cinema which does not suppress the process of narration but rather subverts it to make it more productive, and thus enriches it.

Culture is the minimum; avant-garde is the maximum. It is needed to give the the the cinematic art a new form... The experimental sector of the radical cinema — which develops political problems in place of reproducing a message codified already in another language — is obviously avant-garde, as are TV features on some painters, inasmuch as the transgression of barriers between one art and another very often leads to the enrichment of the domain of different arts and to the enlargement of the range of possibilities.[9]

Relations between education and culture often lead to the academisation of culture, but, actually, it is the opposite that should be welcomed. To introduce live culture into educational activities is to bring life into educational experience. If an educational project is meant to be an implement of training in self-reliance, then the introduction of this life-culture is the precondition for overcoming the present and emerging problems of contemporary societies. The cultural dimension also reinforces individual and collective self-teaching because it allows the self-teachers to continue their education apart from cultural institutions.

The involvement of municipal authorities in the field of culture can assume different aspects, and it is feasible to speak of three kinds of interventions: (a) direct activities, like the encouragement of folk culture and of local languages; traditional and new cultural services (libraries, museums, schools of music, literacy for migrant workers, cultural and educational activities for the unemployed and others); (b) cultural initiatives in conjunction with other structures: schools, work-places, sport centres, mass media; (c) support of cultural activities (prizes, exhibitions, purchases of works of art).

The revolution in communication (extension of television programmes to a 24-hour service, television links through telephone to data banks, to videotapes, etc.) will have consequences for cultural consumption in individual free time. Increasingly, more time will be invested in watching television and in conversing with data-bank services. This revolution in communication will have consequences on educational and cultural consumption. Local authorities can become engaged with the mass media at the local and regional levels.[10]

Municipal authorities can contribute to the development of cultural life if they stimulate local initiatives, and decentralise their activities through a support of local cultural initiatives (e.g. the civic centres for cultural action in Barcelona) that allow more people to partake in cultural life. The removal of territorial limits to local authority activities also allows activities of a holistic nature where educational action, cultural action, and communication can develop respectively. If municipal authorities can help creative production, without either imposing conditions or muzzling creativity, then cultural action in the city can have a strong reciprocal impact, and creativity will be stimulated by the cultural institutions. In the city and in its districts, creative producers can meet among themselves and establish a dialogue with social, political and cultural movements.

Urban life can contribute either to the struggle against cultural marginalisations or, conversely, to reinforce these marginalisations. In short, culture can contribute to the reproduction or to the democratisation of an existing national or local society. Thus, cultural activities can be beneficial in overcoming discrimination regarding age, sex, initial education, ethnic origin, provided that they create opportunities for mass involvement.

Educational and Cultural Structures and the Rural Environment

If lifelong education policies do not take into consideration the complexity of social and production systems they may become the instrument for the strengthening of social inequalities instead of democratisation. We cannot avoid this problem when considering education and rural schools. Even if we tend to generalise about their homogeneous character, from the sociological point of view, rural, urban or suburban environments are not always so. That is why it is necessary for education structures to know in advance the reality of those different environments.

In many countries the following may characterise young and adult populations in rural areas:

- a gradual reduction of per cent of workers involved in agriculture
- a growing percentage of female and aged population
- a combining of employment in agriculture and other industry, especially in countries rapidly industrialising.

The present and future changes in the socio-economic spheres of the rural environment (agricultural reforms, different organisation of production, relations between production and market sales, dialectic relations between changes in production structures and improvement of social and cultural infrastructures and vice-versa) are rarely linked with ideas concerning educational policies and practice. Professional or pre-professional training not taking into account these changes could become insignificant for the needs of the country or region.

In the purely economic evaluation of educational results it is easy to misjudge the results of educational reforms and policies. The GNP (and it is also difficult to judge how much education contributes to the growth of the GNP) is an important though not sufficient indicator. The qualitative as well as the quantitative dimensions should be considered in the evaluation of educational results. Such evaluation is even more difficult when the choice of these indicators implies a choice between educational policies and the development of societies.

The choice of objectives, indicators and evaluation criteria by the population is the key point in an educational policy based on their creative participation in educational projects on national and local scales. Partnership planning in the field of education and the collective management of educational structures are probably one of the possible ways which would permit a solution to the crisis of both the values and inadequacies of education facilities in our times.

The new internal and international balances, technological changes, the capital costs of investments in industry and some infrastrusture often reduce the percentage of the population involved in manufacture and create the social and economic gap between 'productive' and 'non-productive' workers. Rural populations also face this problem because land reform and industralisation change the stucture of the working population. The solution to problems concerning the working population in various countries have to be found through economic and social policies, but education can help these policies. Changes at the level of production, social and cultural structures (or simply creation of such structures) are in many cases the result of the dependence of the country on urban environmental and administrative structures. The reciprocal influence of such changes and, at the same time, a time factor in agricultural production and rural life have to be taken into consideration while introducing such changes. Therefore, qualifications are needed not only in technology but also in the social and cultural dimension of new production structures; qualifications for various categories of existing and new services coherent with and relevant to socio-economic reality, preparation to the new forms of individual and collective life. The objectives are often forgotten by educational structures, which are developed at the quantitative level but are not flexible at the qualitative one.

The existence of a wide educational sphere such as the rural environment offers great possibilities for exploitation, but not only of its natural environment. The rich social, cultural, scientific and technological experience of this environment is often neglected by educational structures. It is also necessary to notice the management of the formal educational sphere represented by the school, library and other educational facilities — if they exist. In this formal sphere there is often a lack of laboratories, workshops, and meeting places which would permit the shaping of collective experience inside the school building, and above all for activities involving the entire population on a regular basis in a permanent way. Of course, the school is not the only privileged place of communal life.

Education in rural areas is often limited to school. This school, together with the teachers, may and often do play roles which surpass their teaching functions (contacts with parents, literacy programmes, etc.). But on the whole, the organisation of schools seems to be centred on traditional education. In this rural context adult education, general and professional, has often very limited possibilities for development. That is why the gap between the generations is even bigger here then in the urban milieu.

A community school in a rural area does not automatically mean changes in structure, content and methods to make it different, but it requires proper relevance to the particular needs of the rural population. For example, technical education cannot ignore existing scientific and technological innovation, physical education should not neglect the possibilities offered by the local environment, or the educational methodology cannot ignore the existing traditions of local communal and co-operative work.

What are the specific contributions of agricultural work to educational experience? Should school experiences in productive work be limited only to agriculture? An answer should be given to these questions in order to avoid the situation in which a community school in a rural area signifies the creation of parallel structures inside one education system. On one hand, it is necessary to develop the experience of agricultural work as part of overall eduacation where manual work is only one element: manual work, scientific knowledge relating to production (biology, zoology, chemistry, botany, physics, etc.) and management (mathematics, accountancy, economy, sociology, management, etc.); on the other hand, maximum effort should be made to place agricultural work within the context of future development. Other experiments in productive work — industrial or in the service sector services — should also be considered (in most countries an important percentage of children currently living in rural areas will move to towns in the future and undertake non-agricultural work): experiences in community services (schools, hospitals, libraries, cultural production and distribution, protection of forests, etc.); experience in light industries; experience in traditional and modern handicraft. The relevance of these work experiences to other educational activities is a necessary and complementary one.

In order to be really useful for educational and social, and not only for 'moral', purposes productive work requires positive relations to be fostered between the school and its environment. The adult population can play an important role in this because it is mostly the non-teacher adults who can contribute to the education of both pupils and teachers and promote productive work.

The relations between school and other educational structures with their natural, social and cultural environment is the key to the whole policy and practice of lifelong education. This relation is not necessarily included into the hypothetical ideal of an 'educated society' but in the dialectic relations existing in the work-place and in social life, where man fights for self-expression and reacts to surroundings which often seek to limit his opportunities for creativity, individual and collective production.

Community Development

In defining and discussing the concept of 'community development', its own universal nature has possibly had a limiting effect: this universality is divorced from the specifics of the various aspects of 'community development' and from the cultural context. One of the first things to be done is to see 'community development' alongside the different cultural demands expressed within contemporary societies. In addition, it is necessary to clarify the distinction between community development and adult education, a notion to which it is often opposed.

In these last few years, community development and adult education have been conceived of as representing collective expression and the militant spirit, on the one hand, and individual expression, private life and the aesthetic dimension on the other. Specific professional training, on the one hand; general development and gratuitous experimentation, on the other.

But today, what are the boundaries of and the prospects for 'community development' and adult education in an urban and industrial setting? The complexities often terrify those who are responsible for initiatives in this area, and thus lead to restricted definitions and practices.

The social, aesthetic, ideological, educational and political objectives of education and 'community development' often confront educationalists and professional developers who are ill-prepared to respond to them. Above all, a restricted interpretation of 'community development' and 'cultural expression' is to be avoided. Cultural facilitators can come from a wide variety of persons and organisations, eg. the managing director of a theatrical empire, the theatre manager, the artist, the poet, the political militant, the critic, journalist, the local administrator. There are two sorts of 'facilitator' — the grass-roots facilitator and the specialist. The task of the former is to be in constant and direct contact with a particular social group where living conditions and specific characteristics are known to him/her first-hand as a result of methodical and well-planned research. The latter is characterised by his/her high degree of competence within a specific cultural area, and by his ability to analyse the characteristics peculiar to each social group. He/she seeks to create a real rapport between his/her own area of expertise and the group with whom he/she is dealing. Nevertheless, the competence and the interests of the grass-roots facilitator often predominate over the wider consideration of 'community development' despite the different sectors less or well known to him/her. Work, leisure, place of residence, place of work, outings; art, science and technology; social life, political life and emotional life — facilitators find themselves working in varied situations, and with individuals whose interests and needs are very different in nature. There is, there-fore, a necessity to work collectively towards 'community develop-ment' using the different contributions of professional and amateur facilitators alike.

The acceptance by educational and cultural bodies of the concept of 'community development' is a step forward, but rarely is 'community development' an instrument of growth and diffusion; often it is little more than a mere listening post'. Schools accept 'community devel-opment' but are often prevented from fostering and lasting develop-ment. Associations which have the expertise to deal with certain areas could become instruments of 'community development'; but are often neither prepared to face problems that go beyond their area of exper-tise, nor willing to apply the concept of 'community development' to their own internal practice. For example, such associations may accept the need to foster the development of workers in their free time, but have difficulty accepting the idea of the 'developing worker' in the place of work, or even in the trade union.

The local and specific nature of education and of a 'community development' can become limiting when it is not related to events beyond the community. Wider objectives, more ambitious 'self-reli-ance', forms of expression which concern all groupings of people, the region and the state are important if one is not to promote those types of 'community development' and education which, in the long term, reinforce existing cultural and educational discrimination. Professional associations, which are indeed an important instrument of 'community development', can also become the basis of dependence and external control. Indeed, it would be dangerous to 'decentralise' the different democratic forms of association life to the extent that, collectively, they have no voice at national level. The new forms of 'development' which are aimed at children, teenagers, adults and senior citizens, are developing spontaneously within educational establishments, within leisure complexes, within spa centres. It would be worth evaluating these new forms of 'community development' and identifying the types of people who initiate such development.

The number of areas, the degree of public involvement and the volume of community development have increased and could increase further, and in certain respects could be better integrated. The demand for theatre, music, sport and physical outlets in general, for science and for everyday technology is growing, but often the bodies best suited to respond to this need are incapable of so doing. What poor examples of cultural development are offered by schools which, in certain areas, are the only places available for public use. What are the difficulties encountered by teachers who are prepared to take the risk, at their own expense, of fostering such development within their own classes; and perhaps even more difficult, fostering a collective self-development among their colleagues? What disparity is there between cultural development in the official centres of 'community development' and the spontaneous development which is created during leisure time? And yet development within institutions and by institutions is a road which should be followed; demand will not be satisfied by spontaneous initiatives alone.

But what type of facilitators are now emerging in the factories, from within educational and cultural establishments, from within communal life? Happily, life seems to be ever vigorous despite the inertia of establishments and the delay of the specialists. An increasingly important area of know-how is being spread by facilitators who are neither teachers nor professional community workers. For instance, in sport and music, young people are following an 'apprenticeship' which deeply influences their development, even though the players are not professionally trained. The same is true for adults in other aspects of community life. These facilitators have developed without specialist guidance and are not usually well received by the 'establishment'; these 'specialist' facilitators are often very shy, lack confidence, and are not

96   *Culture and Community Development*

used to their full potential. Too often, it is the pedants and the administrators (the professionals) who dominate the activities of 'community development'.

Industrialised societies (as well as the majority of already developing societies) can find in culture important answers to the problem of their organisation and survival. There is a reluctance to tackle local, natural and international problems, with all their psychological, social and economic dimensions, and this failure results in entrenchment, violence, meaningless repetition of activities and a loss of meaning and purpose in life. The re-orientating of the objectives of industrialised societies to establish new and more equitable relationships between the different social groups means above all that education must be given a priority role in daily life; and it must be an education composed of knowledge, of discovery, of curiosity, and of the transforming of the self and of one's environment. Viewed in this way, education can become the true indicator of development.

Notes

1. United Nations, *The World Population Situation in 1983*, New York, United Nations, 1984
2. E. Lebas, (ed.) (and the contributions of E. Mingione, V. Granados, G. Andriusz), 'Urban and Regional Sociology in Advanced Industrial Society: a Decade of Marxist and Critical Perspectives', *Current Sociology*, no. 1, Spring 1982
3. I. Biealecki and J. Sikorska, 'In the Sphere of Human Needs and Aspirations', *Sisyphus Sociological Studies*, Warsaw, 1982
4. M.-T. Sirvent, *Leisure Time, Popular Culture and Education in Urban Periphery of Latin American Cities*, Vitoria, Brazil, 1982, mimeo
5. 'Dossier Bercy', *Opus international*, Summer 1982, 13-26
6. G. Naud, 'Les lieux affinataires de la culture populaire à Québec', *Intervention*, Québec, June 1982 15/16, 4-11
7. F. Mahler, 'Aspirations et créativité sociale' in P.H.Chombart de Lauwe, *Transformations sociales et dynamique culturelle*, Paris, CNRS
8. Union Générale des Travailleurs Sénégalais en France, *Barrage: développement ou sous-développement*, Paris, 1982
9. R. Prédal, 'Aujourd'hui, l'avant-garde', *Cinémaction*, no. 10-11, 1980, 310
10. Auteurs variés, 'Les radios municipales', *Arrel*, Apr.-Sept. 1982, Barcelona

8 MIGRATION AND CREATIVITIES

The literature concerning migrant workers often reflects the viewpoint of institutions and governments: it is only to a limited extent the expression of the migrant workers themselves. An effort to understand the perspective of migrant workers on the question of emigration is needed for the development of policies and activities which respond to the needs, demands and expectations of migrant workers. This would permit the removal of this issue from a purely economic approach based on the profitability of these workers, on the one hand, and from sentimentalism, pity and paternalism, on the other.

The rights of workers to migrate and to circulate freely have already been defended by a trade unionist.[1] Throughout their own history, workers' movements in industrial countries have learned that these two rights are important. To deny them to workers coming from the most marginal countries today would be contradictory and, in the end, against the interests of workers as a whole.

Education for migrant workers is but one dimension of an issue that extends beyond literacy training and educational assistance both for the workers and for their families. Within this larger framework, education can play one of several roles. The central question is: which shall it be, education to reinforce relationships of dependence in the countries of origin or of reception, or else positive discrimination in preparation for a new world order of education? This new world order would be one in which migrant workers would not only be among the beneficiaries but to which they would also make a full contribution.

It is through the rediscovery of the histories of education and of culture that a response to the question about education can emerge. The definition of the culture and the educational traditions of migrant workers requires research extending well beyond the easily obtained bibliography. It is a question of studying publications often poor in means but rich in content; of discovering experiences lived but not written down and about the bringing to light of collective knowledge whose creative and provocative powers at present discourage conservative publishing houses and disturb the mass media. To seize upon and utilise the richness of the culture of migrant workers could mean the development of fruitful intercultural relations for the different countries concerned. Migrants arrive not only with a need for work but also with experience, hope and a receptive openness to change. Migrant workers, sometimes by necessity, sometimes by their own choice, are often individuals who are open and amenable to cultural exchange and communication.

Popular conceptions of the status and condition of migrant workers change when they are perceived as cultural representatives and not merely as individuals in search of work. The development of their countries of origin, the discovery of natural reserves with the possibility of controlled exploitation and new international relations all affect the conditions and status accorded to these workers. But must the countries which receive these workers await these changing attitudes before beginning to realise that these workers are individuals with knowledge, with a contribution to make and a desire to participate in the development of their countries of origin, which often rejected them, and of the countries in which they have come to work, countries which also often seem to reject them.

Although emigration on a wide scale is not a new phenomenon, it is still assuming impressive dimensions. On the one hand, it is important to recall that in Europe, there were already 800,000 immigrant workers in Germany in 1907, and that around 15 per cent of the population of Switzerland consisted of immigrant workers in 1910. By 1886 France had already experienced the presence of 1 million immigrant workers.[2] On the other hand, emigration, often related to the diffusion of technology and capital, is rapidly becoming general throughout the world and no longer concerns only the industrial countries.

We are also witness to two other phenomena which are linked to that of emigration but are classified under different titles: the growth in the number of refugees and the establishment of economic enclaves controlled to a great extent from the outside. The number of refugees is increasing at an impresssive rate, and often their conditions are deteriorating for lack of organization and preparation for their reception and for the failure to provide work. In some cases it is difficult to differentiate between migrant workers and refugees. The world's refugees already total several million, with Africa being the continent where the phenomenon is the most extensive.[3]

In the case of economic enclaves, there are workers who remain in their own countries but who, in a certain sense, are migrant workers. Their working conditions, their contracts, their career possibilities and their professional future are not dependent on decisions reached within their own country, but on decisions that are made by the different financial and industrial groups which control the 'decentralised' industries and commerce for which they work.

Maybe within the hostility toward and rejection of migrant workers there is a subconscious feeling that we can all become 'migrants', either rich or poor. Mobility between regions and within the productive system is accelerating, and is affecting a larger and larger number of workers. In fact, in the future, education concerning the problems of emigration will have a field of action much more extensive than that existing today. The public of such education in effect includes all populations: on the one hand, more and more migrants are asking for training programmes; on the other hand, all native populations need to be educated towards intercultural exchange, for international migration and for ending of all forms of racism.

For education, then, the phenomenon of migration, rather than remaining exceptional, is in the process of becoming a permanent condition. It follows that a new attitude is needed on the part of instructors and students toward migration: this process could contribute to enriching the content of educational structures which are today in search of new guiding principles. The transformation of monocultural into intercultural institutions requires both the expansion and opening up of educational institutions, and the stimulation of new forms of training for new and traditional publics. The task is not easy since, for the moment, educators have only limited means at their disposal with which to pursue intercultural activities that are inspired by the idea of greater justice in international relations between and within different countries.

The human sciences have often forgotten or, worse, have studied the most peripheral societies and marginal groups only from a racist and class-based perspective. Intercultural research can be an instrument for perpetuating dependency or, on the contrary, for stimulating the 'indigenisation' of the human and social sciences.

A knowledge of migrants, both historical and contemporary, is necessary. Native populations often express fear of and sometimes even disdain towards the mannerisms of immigrants: their collective identity, style of dress, attitude toward money, and perspectives on life and death.[4] To train oneself to accept different forms of self-expression is a concern of native and immigrant populations alike. Maybe the point of departure for both the acceptance of the mannerism of others and the development of more rational impressions is the liberation of individuals from their own fears and fantasies.

If the relationship between nationals and immigrants is on a basis of equity, education and culture will no longer be products only to be given or sold to immigrants. They, like all other citizens, will have a right to culture and to education, with the avant-garde also included. They will be able to take part in political life, in cultural life creation, in production, in communication. Why should inferior educational and cultural facilities always be the lot of the most marginal?

The observation of reality shows us otherwise: among other things, cultural life is enriched, and often to a great extent also represented, by creative people who come from the outside. Relationships that are more just have their basis in the rights of association and of communication of underprivileged populations, rights that are closely linked to the right to work, in its individual and collective dimension.

The politics of immigration do not vary according to cultural or humanitarian logics. It is economic and demographic laws that inspire them: integration, assimilation, or repatriation.[5] Within the framework of these different choices, one can have policies that are racist or that, on the contrary, are open to immigrant populations. Educational activities reflect the policies adopted and also the goals that are sought as a result of those choices. Policies oriented toward repatriation indicate only the desire to be rid of foreign workers but, on the contrary, others can foster joint economic and cultural co-operation between those countries concerned with the stabilising of human resources and with reinforcing co-operation. Policies of integration can indicate more than a formal respect for other cultural traditions; they can result in real co-operation taking into consideration the particular qualities of different cultures and resulting in genuine interaction between them. Whether assimilation is free or imposed is significant: immigrant individuals and groups can choose a level of integration of a high order through an identification with the culture of their own country, or else can be subject to a process of assimilation which results in the disappearance of their own cultural traditions, of their ethnic identity, and of their ways of thinking and of living.

Continuing observations on the evolution of native and immigrant populations, in relation to the labour market as well as participation in educational and cultural life, are necessary for the planning of new policies concerning emigration.

All generalisations concerning the politics of migration are to be avoided in view of the dynamic nature of the populations concerned: demographic analyses reveal that, after a period of settlement, even if the number of workers diminishes, the active population can increase as a result of the changing relationship of women to the world of work, of the entry of the children of immigrant workers into the labour market, and of fluctuations in the average age and of the shift movement of workers to the tertiary sector of production.[6]

If it is true that education cannot change the world of work, it is true all the same that education can reinforce the possibilities of access to the labour market and that it can contribute to the creation of employment. But migrant workers suffer additionally to the extent that there remain other difficulties of access to training: the limited available means and their uncertain relationship to professional careers, and the lack of interest of those responsible for work and for training in the face of the demands for education from migrant workers.[7]

If, in general, workers find themselves at a loss in the face of automation and computerisation and their consequences on employment, immigrant workers find themselves in an even more precarious situation. One can ask whether education can help workers profit from new technologies or whether it can only help to prepare them to suffer its consequences.

The speed of economic and technological change, as well as of demographic dynamics, are of consequence for emigration and immigration. Countries that are exporters of work become importers of work. Demographic increases or decreases make immigrants either indispensable or a 'surplus' to the economies of countries. But can one reduce individuals or populations to the status of objects of exchange, of which others profit in times of need and free themselves in times of plenty?

If the creation of work is linked to the creativity of workers and consumers,[8] immigrant workers could very well contribute with their knowledge, their taste for risk, their need for identity and their motivation for creation and production. Native populations free themselves from prejudices toward migrant workers when they realise that, often, in the past as well as in the present, these workers have contributed to periods of expansion, of creativity and of development within lost countries.

The centrality of education and production of knowledge to the productive process can have negative consequences for all those who are marginal to productive activities. Thus, there is the necessity for policies oriented toward the right to work,[9] a right which is closely linked with the right to education. It follows that there is also the need for policies capable of rapidly integrating young people in the productive process. The wastage of the energy of young people who leave school for years of unemployment and, in certain countries, also a prolonged military service, is no longer tolerable. The young people have the right to contribute and to participate in productive life without losing years in fruitless endeavour to find work which is in itself a state of progressive degradation. The second generation of migrant workers is often more affected by this condition due to the system of formal education, which is often discriminatory, and to an industrial system in which there is a demand not only for professional qualification but often for 'the right type' of recruits. A full exploitation of human resources means the recognition of the knowledge gained through work and self-education; this recognition would permit the opportunity to gain scientific and technological qualifications, notably among immigrant workers of the first generation, whose contribution to culture and to the development of the country where they live are not given due recognition.

The state on the one hand, and trade union on the other, can both contribute to the development of new relationships between migrant and native workers. At first sight there appears to have been some delay on both sides. The rights of emigration and of immigration have not become generalised in all countries under the pretext of protecting the interests of native workers. But maybe, in the long run, the interests of foreign and national workers are closely linked: in effect, unity stimulates the participation of foreign workers in trade union life.

The case of young people who do find work and, as a result, often join trade unions, is similar; the entry of young people into productive life means the extension of unionisation to them. A trade union with the narrow objective of being concerned only with the rights of its active workers, contains in itself reasons for its own potential crises.

The problem of migrant workers is closely linked to that of the right to work: it seems that certain categories of workers, in relation to age, sex, geographic origin, are penalised more than others in societies in which the right to work does not seem to exist or is no longer respected. The rights to work, to peace and to the general respect of the individual and collective rights of man seem to be becoming the fundamental objectives upon which young people in the North and South, in the East and West, wish to lay claim.

Are conclusions possible? By way of example, it is possible to point to certain short-, medium- and long-term solutions:

· Migrant workers can constitute a group of intermediaries in North-South relations in surmounting their conditions of marginality.
· Their involvement trade union activities could be accomplished, above all, by their direct participation in union life and not

through the defence of their rights by others.
· The most detailed information possible should be given to migrant workers on opportunities for training.
· The increased participation of immigrant workers at the level of political, union and administrative life would perhaps be the most advanced form of adult education, and would encourage the involvement of migrant workers in the economic and social politics that concern them.
· The integration of migration workers, and notably of the second generation, on the basis of equality does not exclude policies of positive discrimination to permit the improvement of the conditions of the underpriviliged which weigh heavily on the professional and social destiny of these workers.
· Research into social, cultural and educational matters is necessary, notably regarding the relationships and changes in the world of work — in effect, these are of consequence for the social conditions of migrant workers. All the same, it would still be necessary to prevent the education of migrants from becoming an area of expensive growth in formal education where eventually the content becomes of little relevance to the workers or simply a new theme for academic debate:
· The realisation of these objectives is conditional, on the one hand, upon the willingness of host countries which receive these workers to be open, and on the other hand, on opportunities for these workers to express themselves through their own organisations and to become actively involved in the matters that concern them.[10] The success and the creativity of these organisations are indicators of the openness of a society. In effect, repression, racism and indifference toward these organisations gives rise to defence mechanisms which are neither beneficial, to migrant workers nor to the societies in which they work.

To liberate oneself from demagogy and a false humanitarianism, and to open oneself to intercultural communication requires from educators a profound self-examination of their own training and their present activities.

Notes

1. E. Vercellino, '400 mila stranieri a lavoro nero', *Rassegna sindacale* 22 October 1977 (cited in *Esperienze e proposte*, no. 38, 1979)

104   *Migration and Creativities*

2. United Nations, *International Migration Policies and Programmes, A World Survey*, New York, 1982, p. 20

3. Various authors, 'Les réfugiés dans le monde', *Problèmes politiques et sociaux*, no. 455, La docujmentation française, 14 January 1983

4. T. Allal, J.P. Bufford, M. Marié, T. Regazzola, *Situations migratoires*, Paris, Editions Galilée, 1977

5. J.P. de Caudemar, *Mobilité du travail et accumulation du capital*, Paris, Maspero, 1976

6. OECD, *Situation présente et évolution probable de l'emploi et fonctionnement des marchés du travail*, 1982

7. J. Riz, *Du secours aux associations de migrants pour la formation*, Paris I, ISST, 1983, mimeo

8. L.C. Pasinetti, *Structural Change and Economic Growth*, Cambridge, University Press, 1981

9. M. Rustin 'A Strategy for Jobs', *New Left Review*, January-February 1983

10. UGTSF, *Migration-Education-Développement*, Paris, 1984

9 EMERGING CULTURAL AND EDUCATIONAL NEEDS

In defining educational programmes there is often a tendency to think of society as it was or as it is, but not of the process of its construction and evolution. Therefore, there is often a lack of relevance in many educational activities. Although potential learners, young and old, are being deceived, they are more sensitive to future trends and perspectives than are the educational institutions themselves. Education for what! Often we ignore the fact that the goals, as well as the contents and methodologies of education, are changing. From management to self-management of productive, community, cultural, social, educational structures; revaluation of the objectives of industrialised society; reorientation of work and social life now fragmented by the international, national and social division of labour; these are some of the objectives present in the dynamics of our society that are demanding very intense educational activities. The new self-management trends require the acquisition of knowledge, skills and new learning in the scientific, technological, economic and social domains. This knowledge requires the acquisition of new learning that is often absent in school programmes and in adult education. It is even more difficult to find educational content capable of helping to reorient the objectives of industrialised societies. These societies are facing major programmes of conversion (in the workplace, in daily life, in geographical mobility, for example). This conversion does not signify a regression solely towards the satisfaction of the basic needs of survival, i.e. safe food, water, clothing and lodging. On the contrary, in this conversion of objectives the satisfaction of qualitative needs is also fundamental.[1] These latter needs concern questions of the quality of life as conceived in different cultures and social groups. In fact, the satisfaction of individual and collective needs in the domain of culture, of mental and physical health and in social relationships can enable our societies to reorient their perspectives for production, consumption and the organisation of work. New ways of thinking about integration between general training and technological and vocational training, as well as new relationships between education and work, appear when young people and adults decide to educate themselves, not only for production, but also to live in more meaningful ways.

The evolution of the educational and cultural demands of workers is sometimes better understood and registered by commercial leisure organisations than by educational and cultural institutions, even in those affiliated to workers' organisations. In industrialised society there is a rising standard of living, a longer period of schooling; the development of a technology to which workers themselves contribute in a very relevant way, and from which they profit unequally. The differing extent to which workers exercise power and control within the productive processes affects their ability to use technological developments to their own advantage.[2]

The inability of educational and cultural structures, and often even of workers' organisations, to understand this evolutionary process prevents workers from profiting from new cultural experiences which could develop within a collective framework. Belonging to a working-class movement can become, because of this cultural gap, merely sentimental and mythical.

New knowledge, new skills, new patterns of behaviour are the concern of important sections of the work-force, both for indigenous and migrant workers, but policies formulated on their behalf are often based on traditional images of the working class that do not take into consideration their changing condition and needs. A worker, who by his own individual effort or by collective work, achieves higher cultural, scientific and economic levels, may have difficulty in finding new educational and cultural experiences that correspond to his own level of development. Current educational structures seem to be insensitive to these new publics and therefore do not provide them with significant educational programmes. The reaction can be either cultural marginalisation (sometimes as a result of traditional working-class attitudes), adaptation to the cultural models fostered by the mass media and/or a purely personal choice of consumption so far as culture, education and leisure are concerned.

Institutions in initial as well as in further education are often slow to recognise the emergence of new clientele so far as educational and cultural activities are concerned. The image that they present of this section of society is the one with which they themselves wish to label it. A new working class is emerging from the contradictions of economic development in industrialised societies; workers share new values concerning the relative importance and meaning of work and leisure. There is a substantial difference between the present living conditions of the older generation compared with their previous working conditions, but these new realities are scarcely perceived by educational and cultural institutions.[3]

It is quite difficult for educators to reach an equilibrium between the precision of educational demand and needs and the general nature of cultural and educational policies. The emergence of new demands and the changes in those already made to educational institutions make this even more difficult. The transition from the need to acquire linguistic knowledge at the primary level (literacy) to the need to master foreign languages or advanced sciences and technology has happened and is now no longer open to debate in this generation. The same person can transform himself from a demander of a very elementary initial training to a demander of higher education within a very few years.

Because of the delay in recognising the rate of individual, as well as collective evolution, a paradoxical situation develops in which we see, on the one hand, cultural and educational facilities which no one wants and on the other, a population which has difficulties in finding cultural and educational institutions which correspond to their demand. For this reason a risk of cultural regression, a gap between the new economic and social possibilities and the educational and cultural development at individual and collective levels, can be foreseen.

The coexistence of the formal and non-formal sectors of the labour market, the segmentation of the labour market within the same formal sector, increases the quality of production from a scientific and technological point of view and leads to the existence of both a skilled and unskilled labour forces. This results either in the speeding up of change, or of retrogression to new and old-type social classes. Educational and cultural institutions are slow to acknowledge these changes. Such institutions perpetuate themselves in the name of pursuing internal procedures.

Any study of the educational needs of workers can become abstract if it is not situated within the concrete, subjective perception and objective development of working-class conditions.[4] It is in relation to this development that the ideologies (and cultural and linguistic needs) of the workers can become diffused. Often, however, the education of workers loses the sense of concrete historical reality and addresses itself to the abstract reality of the 'ideal worker' who is motivated, collectively orientated, knows his place, and is deferential to his superiors!

Sometimes we forget the consequences of technological innovation on training.[5] A considerable change in basic training seems to be necessary. In the past, it was the principle of a stable specialisation that was required. Now, under the influence of the technical and scientific revolutions, another principle, that of maximal adaptation to changing conditions, has appeared.[6] In the past, as tasks and related technology evolved, workers were always in learning situations, and there was a permanent progression in the acquisition of new skills and in the replacement of tools and machines.[7] Nowadays, the acquisition of and development of individual and collective, social and technical knowledge is restricted. Those not working in research at a very high level or in some craft sectors, cannot always make progress in their own jobs, because it is difficult either to improve their instruments or invent new production techniques.[8] Working conditions are not always stimulating or creative, or permitting of individual worker initiative.

People with no continuity in their formal education encounter difficulties in their relationships with the educational system; they are disappointed after training because they do not see any change in their working conditions. For this reason it is very important to maintain a continuous link between work and education and not to restrict the scope of training, but to enable some positive dialectic relationships between training and the worker, even within the framework of existing constraints. Such training should go beyond the limited goals of traditional vocational training.

The difficulties and the crises of working relationships have their special characteristics. Often, to understand the complexity of these social relationships it is necessary to look beyond the objective problems and to seek out the underlying motivations guiding apparently similar actions. The flight from work is a case in point. We have to be careful not to group together all heterogeneous phenomena under the title of 'allergy to work'. First of all, we have the plight of exploited workers facing very arduous conditions of work and who, for example, attempt to escape from the factory production line. This is a very important manifestation of class conflict. But there are also much more ambiguous phenomena that find their origin in some social groups belonging to the tertiary sector of production. In the name of creativity they resist all the constraints of work and seek every opportunity to escape from them. This can be fine, even honourable, but it is not likely to succeed in overturning today's production relationship.[9]

These remarks allow us to avoid any generalisations concerning the attitudes and educational and cultural interests of workers. The idea that education is not simply an expense, but that it can become productive and, consequently, that educators and students are workers like others[10] can be accompanied by the hypothesis that workers are all potential students. Lifelong education projects attempted up to now are but a poor manifestation of this hypothesis.

One of the major problems that young people and adults have to face in the educational system is mobility within the system itself. In some cases social selection and educational selection combine with the inertia of the educational system. In other cases younger and adult students are kept in educational streams because there is no communication between the different educational sectors. In yet more cases, and mainly in adult education, a distribution of resources does not always correspond to these demands. A regulation of the educational system is possible through reforms within its own structures and/or through changes in the social-class system. Greater internal coherence of the educational system can be achieved through the continuous training of personnel of different types — professional and volunteer, permanent and temporary. The social-class system is affected by qualitative and quantitative demographic dynamics which also disturb existing educational systems; these need to be sufficiently flexible to adapt themselves to new realities like age, level of initial schooling, geographical origin and the particular jobs of young people and adults. The lack of adaptability of educational systems leads to crises and stagnation within them; and this results in rising costs, the exclusion of certain groups and a taking over of the provisions of training by the productive system itself.

The facility of educational programmes, positive in itself, becomes negative when young people and adults do not see any progress in their learning. There are, on the one hand, school and university courses which end in the award of diplomas, and on the other, knowledge whose acquisition is not recognised and is of a fragmentary nature. This does not mean that youth and adult education has to be formalised, but that new ways have to be found to coordinate better the different forms of learning which make them complementary and progressive.

Society acclaims the virtues of education yet at the same time the educational system, as a purely cost-benefit exercise, selects an elite of students, dissuading the majority remainder from aspiring to its highest levels. The reluctance of some firms to pay adequate salaries to their holders discourages certain types of qualification, and the lack of prospects discourages and limits educational investment (of individuals and of the corporation). The question should be that of the individual's right to work but not always that of the right to a higher level of work because he has had a higher level of education. The cost of creating a job in modern society is rising rapidly in some sectors.

The development of education is a positive fact in many countries, but this development occurs largely in those areas where the gaining of a higher education diploma is associated with a corresponding type of work. Within this perspective of the development of education this equation is no longer possible; either access to higher education has to be limited, or it has to be accepted that this equation is not automatic, or that rotation of tasks has to be developed. Possibly, this third option in one way or another (job rotation, reduction of working hours, recurrent education and training, using workers as educators, the cultural enrichment of leisure time, overcoming the social and to some extent the sexual division of labour which is in itself a result of technicial specialisation, the enlargement of general education beyond a purely vocational purpose, etc.) is the most promising; but it does imply changes in social and productive relationships.

Psychological and interpersonal problems exist in every society, whether they are rapidly changing or very conservative societies. The individual and collective solutions to these problems are in themselves educative and cultural, but there is still a reluctance to deal with those problems which give rise to ignorance, intolerance, racial discrimination and violence.

New educational and cultural curricula are necessary both for young people and adults: highly educated young people and adults, and the establishment of new certificate-granting educational systems are not sufficient. Both young people and adults seek continuity in their quest for knowledge and its application in their daily lives. Very often, however, the educational and cultural activities proposed have no such continuity, unless they are viewed strictly in their relation to university and school patterns. Building up a new, well-structured, educational and cultural programme demands intense effort. Any failure, caused by the irrelevance or inaccessibility of the new educational curricula can create a resistance toward further innovation, and in some cases lead to reactionary stances among the students themselves.

Current cultural and educational action reflect a crisis of established structures and values. Up to now, educational and cultural activities have reflected the structures and values upheld by the wider population. Now, however, they face new and more diverse and critical audiences. Traditional slogans, spiritual values and references no longer provide an appropriate internal framework for educational and cultural activities. The sense of impatience among young people – or their passiveness – are embarrassing to educators and cultural organisers alike. Young people either pose very specific questions or they are silent. A richer and more diverse training is needed, with concrete experiences as the starting point, leading up to advanced theoretical research. Neither despotism nor 'unchangeableness' have meaning within the fields of education and culture. Relevance, flexibility and adaptability with respect to the contents, methods, structures and timing of education are needed.

For example, overworked workers, or unemployed and underemployed workers are a reality in many countries, but the cultural and educational structures do not take this into account. Educational and structural action can develop at two levels: first, through increased awareness by workers of an area for solidarity; secondly, through the development of educational, cultural and social services capable of unifying, at the social level, those workers who are divided at the level of production.

Even in the face of educational and cultural policies that lead to acculturation, cultural strategies of resistance and innovation are possible. However, in order to succeed, these strategies demand total and in-depth understanding of problems if the difficulties of coherence in their implementation due to lack of means, time, etc. are to be overcome.

The dialectic of education is not situated between institutions and spontaneous action, but rather between evolving and creative activity and those actions which favour dependence and conformity; cultural and educational actions have to lead to a better understanding of oneself, of others and of one's environment and provide the instruments which can be used to transform one's material, cultural and social conditions.

Better relations between culture and education are not always realised in educational practice. The culture that is to be found in educational programmes is often separate from living and daily culture. Oral culture, in particular, is very often forgotten:

It seems to me that we should not separate oral and written culture as if there were populations floating in the sea of written culture. We all have an oral culture, even scholars and scientists. Orality, in itself, is not disassociated from gestures, covering the whole daily life of a population and not only its verbal expressions, its tales, its proverbs, its legends, its recipes, its verbal wisdom, its art and its songs.[11]

Culture in daily life, in work and in leisure: this type of culture is often ignored, even if it is the expression and the creative manifestation of each of us at home, at work, in free time, in social life. Education that helps to locate a person in relation to his environment, taking into account his culture, is an education which requires neither imposition nor facilitation. Nevertheless, literature reflecting this type of culture is rare.[12]

A contemporary analysis of all elements that condition educational processes (new international division of labour, demographic pressures, computer technology, worldwide emigration and immigration, etc.) should stimulate new thinking about education and culture. For example, the cultural and linguistic factors in workers' education are changing rapidly. New relationships between workers of different continents require intense cultural action to prevent the working classes of the industrial countries from accepting the false image that is given them about the people in marginal societies. Better understanding between people may come, but there is still a risk of conflict between workers in industrialised societies and those in marginal countries. Often, demonstrations take place which should cause more concern in the political, cultural and trade union organisations of the working classes in industrial countries. The orientation of workers towards the international context of work is not mechanical: political education is needed to stimulate it. But this orientation towards internationalism is not only a political or an ideological choice − it has to be nourished with a rich cultural content and with a cultural, historical, economic consciousness of different civilisations. In some countries indifference or even hostility towards ethnic groups are evident; very often different standards of living are the main cause, but in other cases, it is purely and simply cultural and social prejudice which makes communication between different ethnic groups impossible.

But what factors can help us to find a new response to the educational and cultural demands of the worker? How can the creativity and cultural desire of the workers be given the opportunity to express themselves? Do they express themselves? There is a tendency to underestimate these questions and to concentrate cultural and educational programmes on moral, ideological and economic objectives only.

Leisure seems to have long been forgotten so far as educational activities are concerned, especially by the intellectuals (who, by the way, are today rediscovering 'private life'). The widespread development of sporting activities has been largely ignored by those responsible for cultural and educational activities. The importance of sports, personal investments of time and money, or travel to see a sporting event, are all manifestations of interest in sport. But international sport can be an occasion for reinforcing ideological dependence, or, on the contrary, for the physical and mental strengthening of individuals. The equilibrium of mental and physical forces, the harmonious development of the body, the maintenance of energy in workers' life and in retirement, can be an important by-product of sport.

Access to educational and cultural centres, which is general in most industrialised societies, is only a preliminary step towards further consolidation. Economic fluctuations still greatly affect the provision of and access to educational and cultural programmes, with 'strict' vocational training being given priority during periods of so-called economic crisis.

Educational and cultural activities are expanding their physical and temporal space, but often public discrimination continues, and marginal people become even more marginal in their access to educational and cultural activities. Cultural and educational stratification is accompanied by stratification of work, of technology and of social relationships. How can this trend be reversed? Within what conceptual framework can an alternative be developed? Should such a conceptual framework ever guide both the hierarchy of education and culture?

Only limited cultural and educational needs are attributed to workers and to families whose work is modest and whose social status is humble. But on what grounds? And why do these prejudices often persist among those who claim, in principle, to have rejected them? Why consider that an unskilled worker, a migrant worker or a peripheral person is satisfied with an education and culture which permit only his physical survival and his acculturation?

Rediscovering and reconstructing educational and cultural space is a cultural activity in itself: the workplace, the municipal and village structure, leisure places, the different expressions of community life can be occasions for cultural and educational development. But often, the representation of 'traditional culture' takes the upper hand and these other possible spaces are neglected. In fact, all aspects of the conservation of nature and of artistic heritage are instruments for cultural identity; any activity leading to this conservation is a cultural activity in itself. New spaces are opening up in leisure, in family life (such as the improvement of the scholastic achievements of children) and in the complexity of working life of some people (and, thus, the levels of vocational training). But what are the cultural and educational propositions which can respond to these new situations? In what way can workers connected with the centres of creation and cultural diffusion participate in the definition of the structures, contents and methods of programmes? Today's urban setting is destroying the traditions of popular cultures, for when facilities for social life and leisure disappear in old districts, they are not always reconstructed in the new ones. New public, educational and cultural centres are being opened, but often without an identity or any cultural approach. At the same time, new folklores are emerging, and the treasures of cultures from distant regions being diffused indirectly through the cultural activities of migrant workers.

There is an increasing gap between researchers, administrators, decision-makers and practitioners in the areas of adult education and cultural action; the results of research and new and original projects are not related to ongoing educational and cultural practices. New ways of thinking about research in adult education, as well as in the training of adult educators are needed; research into the organisation of the state, the economic anthropology of working life, of contemporary economic problems such as inflation, the balance of economic development in the north and the south, unemployment, etc. can be a fundamental part of the training of adult educators. Very often, however, their training programmes do not touch upon these problems. Adult educators, as well as adult learners, need more contact with artists, writers, painters, film-makers and, through these relationships, they can widen their potential for linguistic, scientific and aesthetic expression.

The development and enrichment of non-essential needs, the enlargement of cultural space, the complexity of working life and geographical mobility are only a few of the elements which demand rich linguistic expression by workers. It is in this area of the enrichment of linguistic expression that, perhaps, what educational institutions offer is the most inadequate. The rudiments of linguistics taught at school and the linguistic universe of the family, work and leisure, blend and integrate with the language of television: the variety of languages among migrant workers increases the number of languages and dialects, but not necessarily the vocabulary and use of language or languages. And, in parallel, the artificial language of computers and international languages (i.e. the English language) are the vehicle for new logical and linguistic uniformity. Artists, writers, theatre and cinema actors can be included in these linguistic contractions, and though certainly striving for answers, their research is often very isolated.

Political and cultural movements in many countries have neglected linguistic problems, or perhaps the linguistic expression of these movements reflects a cultural conservatism. Art and literature have often been considered as parallel activities to political action, but are not necessarily integrated into the problems of daily political life.

Linguistic potential, represented by the development of science and technology is often neglected by educators; young people and adults are confronted with much information during their working day, but the education they have received often does not enable them to realise their linguistic potential in reference to it.

Education research and practice requires a wider conceptual framework; for tomorrow's education will stand in relation to today's education as the spaceship does to the bicycle.

Notes

1. A. Heller, 'Un prologo più che un epilogo. Replica sulla teoria dei bisogni e della vita quotidiana', *Aut-Aut*, May-August, 1977

2. R. Kalany, 'La structure des besoins culturels', *Bulletin* no. 5, Institut de recherches culturelles de Croatie, 1978

3. C. Griffin, 'An ideology of needs, access and provision', *Curriculum Theory in Adult and Lifelong Education*, London, Croom Helm, 1983

4. A. Gilly, *La formación de la conscienza obrera en Mexico*, Primer seminario internacional sobre historia del movimiento obrero latino-americano, Caracas, 1979, mimeo

5. Z. Grzelak, *Le niveau de la technique et son influence sur la structure des qualifications professionnelles*, Unesco, IIPE, 1977

6. Ibid.

7. A. Gorz, *Adieux au prolétariat. Au-delà du socialisme*, Paris, Editions Galilée, 1980, pp. 139-40

8. Ibid.

9. 'Entretien avec Pierre Naville sur l'automation et l'avenir du travail', *Critiques de l'économie politique*, Oct.-Dec. 1977, 18

10. Stipe Sugar, *Skola i Tvornica* (School and factory), Pedagoska Biblioteca, Zagreb, 1977

11. A. Stefani, 'Cultures, Ordres et Media' in G. Poujol and R. Labourie (eds), *Les cultures populaires*, INET, 1979, p. 120

12. For example, L. Zanier, *Chez Diaz . . . Us al Meriti*, Piello, Circolo Culturale Colavini, 1976

PART FOUR: EDUCATIONAL TRENDS AND ISSUES:
EXAMPLES OF ACTION, CO-OPERATION AND
CONFLICT

10 TOWARDS A NEW EDUCATIONAL ORDER: ENCOUNTERS AND CONFRONTATION IN EDUCATION

I. Inequality in Education

(1) *The Authorities*

The authorities responsible for educational policy in certain countries are finding themselves confronted with some hard facts. It is anticipated that by 1990 the world's illiterates will total 882 million, i.e. 24.9 per cent of the population over 15 years of age. By the year 2000 the percentage could be reduced to 21.5, but with a real increase in the total numbers to 912 million.[1] With regard to employment, in order to meet the necessary demand for work between now and the year 2000, one billion jobs would have to be created.[2]

State expenditure in the educationsl sphere varies considerably from one country to another in relation to the Gross National Product (GNP) and the entire public expenditure: from 1.3 to 10-12 per cent of the GNP and from 7 to 30 per cent of the entire state expenditure. The developing countries (with a few exceptions) cannot devote the same percentage of their GNP to educational programmes as the industrialised countries; hence the importance in developing countries; of non-formal education, which remains the only form open to a large portion of their populations.

(2) *Scarcity of Education in Some Countries and 'Educational Surplus' in Others*

In some of the industrialised countries the real problem for young and old is not access to education, but rather, choosing a satisfactory alternative from among the possibilities offered. There is still a sector of the population in the industrialised countries not properly informed, and without easy access to educational institutions. On the other hand, in some countries where financial resources for education are limited, institutional educational provision is still scarce; in other words, impossible for certain groups who are the most disadvantaged, owing to their social or geographical positions. The construction of new international educational structures might be one of the future tasks of the international community. Activities could be limited to the development of

119

theoretical developments and the promotion of educational experiments, with the possibility left open for decision-making concerning equality in the educational sphere. The United Nations in their resolution 'Educational Rights' (36-152 of 16/12/81) invited all member states to adopt the authorised measures which guarantee the full right to universal education.

(3) Industrialised Countries

In the industrialised countries the least favoured communities — those involved in internal and external migration — are given (even if to a limited degree) the possibility of assistance in their development. There is also a guarantee of support for their infrastructures (social, sanitary, educational, etc.) and thus for their educational system even if the local revenues are insufficient. Today, entire countries are faced with the dramatic situation of educating children and young people who emigrate because of lack of work. First and foremost, it will be important to reconsider the national income in relation to national development of communities and countries by the creation and maintenance of infrastructures whenever necessary. Seen in historical perspective this would only be compensatory.

(4) Developing Countries

From countries having a considerable degree of security and offering multiform educational programmes (from primary school to the transition between school and work, and from vocational training to third-age education) we pass on to others whose economic conditions are such that only part of the population can benefit even from primary education, and an even more limited number can have the benefit of a secondary education. Fortunately, neither the level of education nor civilisation reached by a population is identified with school, since the cultural wealth of an individual is not merely measured by his/her command of the alphabet. Lifelong education, in our time, is not only interwoven with the culture of the written word, but with oral, visual and manual culture as well.

To close one's eyes and be oblivious to the wealth of culture and different forms of self-education of people who have received little or no schooling, means the acceptance of a permanent dependence by those who have received either a limited primary education or none at all. When discussing education and work, and education and leisure, one gets the impression that formal education is the only target.

Fortunately, however, adults and young people alike educate themselves at work and through new relationships in their free time via
different kinds of self-study — both individual and collective — thanks
to their different cultural backgrounds.

(5) *Quite Significant Numbers of Various Population Groups Find
Themselves Without a Real Right to Formal Education*

This phenomenon usually strikes non-industrialised countries the worst,
but it is not absent in industrialised countries. People often have a fixed
idea of those who need a basic education. In fact, in modern society
basic education concerns a heterogeneous public and one must not
forget the mobility of this group. Geographical mobility, and the
incessant technological changes and the transfer of production from
one sector to another demand the acquisition of qualifications necessi-
tating a continually advancing basic education.

The relationship between these target groups — young and old —
and the education and training programmes offered by the production
and education systems are often very difficult. These groups are
excluded from the programming of the activities and are often considered more as utilisers than protagonists. One often gets the impression that the educational programmes for this new kind of target group
tend to reveal the desires and dreams of those who make them, rather
than of those for whom they are planned. If it is always necessary for
the participants to attend these educational activities, it is especially
in the preparation of the programmes for these new kinds of participants, who have had little or no education, that this participation is of
vital importance.

(6) *Education in Time of Plenty and of Poverty*

In the 1980s, certain countries and their populations have been trying
to evaluate the results of educational programmes in which they have so
heavily invested in the past. The expansion in the quality of education,
relatively significant during the last 20 years, does not supply a satisfactory answer to the problems of development even if we do not
appreciate its present impact.

II. Changing the Models for Educational and Productive Systems

(1) *General and Vocational Education*

General and vocational education which is becoming a continual learning process in the life of the individual, not only in daily life but also in various institutionalised educational contexts, is a new fact of life which has not yet been fully understood by educators and those responsible for the educational systems.

Lifelong education, whether it is voluntary or compulsory, education developed on scholastic lines or in the work sphere, in social life or in times of employment and unemployment, is a new reality which could require the available educators to take more risks. It will require inventiveness and creativity, and above all a lasting ability to exceed the limits of their own occupation.

Education is not simply a preparation for life; it is becoming a significant part of the majority of man's activities. The passing from one section of production to another, the economic crisis, the restructuring and development in the traditional sectors of production, and the geographical mobility of workers are all situations that require renewed attention in the educational sphere. But most of the time educational systems have not been prepared to use their resources to capacity to face up to these situations.

(2) *Changes in Education*

Radical changes in the systems of production involve great alterations in the educational system, the expansion of which causes duplication elsewhere without necessarily having any connection with the system of production. The new manifestations of power (military, bureaucratic, economic, communicative, etc.) engineer new educational ideologies. There is a perceptible change in actual education, but educational analysis by experts often remains rather traditional.

(3) *New Initiatives*

Open universities, trade unions, industries, vocational education institutions, local authorities, community organisations, the media in general, have been active. They have produced new programmes and have tried to appeal to a new public. But those who avail themselves of these possibilities have often continued to represent the 'traditional' public. In fact, up to the present day, self-directed learning, both individually and in groups, has been the answer for many people and groups who have not found fulfilment within the framework of institutional (formal) education. Industrial countries also find, even in this day and age, that part of their population is illiterate, and it is surprising to find how little self-criticism there is to be found amongst those responsible for the educational system. Unfortunately, in most of these cases, conscience-smitten authorities do not react by putting forward suggestions to remodel the educational system, but rather limit themselves to planning programmes for the illiterate.

(4) *Obstacles to Education – the Educators*

Educators, including adult educators, can sometimes constitute an obstacle to education, and this is not as absurd as it might seem. They dread changes in the educational sphere, in the sense that this will oblige them to reconsider their roles (and in a certain sense the content of their work); they identify education too much with their profession. It can happen, for example, that the organisation of adult education, instead of forming a powerful force for educational development, discourages those who hope for something more creative. Better ways must be found for both general and adult education and more people should be involved; however, the framework should not lead to a separation of those engaged professionally from those who are interested and involved outside their professional activities.

Over-organising educational activities on purely legal and administrative lines can, in certain cases, act as a brake to development. The forces which could act as the beginning of new, more imaginative educational activities often stumble on unduly strict legal and administrative obstacles. On the other hand, conservative elements make the most of 'frameworks' to restrict and obstruct innovative educational trends.

(5) *Obstacles to Education – Discourse and Rhetoric*

Discourse and rhetoric which do not correspond to educational practice can also obstruct education. It often happens that educational movements refer to some of the verbal traditions that no longer apply to the present-day situation (and this also applies, and is perhaps bound to certain political parties and traditionally progressive trade unions which are, however, engaged in myths and outdated slogans). It is not possible to confine ourselves to referring to working-class traditions without at the same time being aware of the following: new generations doing degrading unappreciated work or having no work; migrant workers (especially the second-generation immigrants); women who are more than ever prepared to face the labour market and who are, in fact, being excluded. Trade unions, political parties and educational movements must be open to the entire population and not only to a certain section. Now that the working class has established itself it cannot be expected to call its weakest members into action. Conservative reactionary powers in industrialised countries are reinforcing their authority, taking advantage of the disunity between the prosperous and those poorly situated in the labour market, and this division also applies to education.

(6) *Cultural Institutions*

A new factor which should be mentioned is that in the industrialised countries and in the Third World a very great interest, especially amongst the young, exists for culture in the broadest sense: theatre, music, circus, sport, etc. But what are the consequences of this growing interest in cultural undertakings? One often gets the impression that certain cultural institutions are protecting themselves from this new trend, indicating that the solution in the future would be to change, as much as possible, even the educational institutions into creative and productive cultural structures. This change must be made, even if one does not know yet how to bring about the transformation in educational structures. People with both creative and productive capacities will have to be placed in the educational and productive systems. The efforts made in our societies for education, health and culture cannot be confined to an exclusive quantitative reinforcement of the existing social, cultural and educational institutions. Continuing on this course would only tend to increase the incompetence of both human and financial resources which are already limited.

(7) *Controls on the System of Education*

It would be a useful exercise to examine the control, either open or hidden, exerted on pupils and educators by (a) formal assessment, (b) the conditions one finds oneself in a career, (c) the lack of information regarding creative educational programmes, a control exercised within the educational and productive systems. Resistance, especially by those further up in the hierarchy, to promoting the education of their subordinates, is common in the various systems and subsystems, i.e. political, economic and cultural. Therefore, subordinates who educate themselves beyond what is required for their jobs disturb the hierarchical power; hence this resistance even in applying certain legislative or contractual decisions designed to promote education for the workers.

Educational regulations are more powerful than one might think and can carry a long way, causing marginalisation, loss of jobs, etc. That is why the different kinds of control and criticism should not be isolated, but form a joint operation giving extensive information within an international plan. (One must also remember that professional literature on education can also be a device for censure.)

Analysis of educational literature reveals that most theoretical and empirical studies are carried out to reinforce the present educational system. It is a fact that literature on education issues from the institutions themselves: research and publications emanate from universities, local authorities, international organisations, industries and trade unions. There is not much entirely impartial literature on this subject. Most of it tends to promote the interests of the institutionalised educational world. One comes across very few empirical studies identifying the causes of dissatisfaction with educational institutions and the desires of people.

International co-operation in the educational sphere could lead to the coordination of effort for new kinds of censure, or on the contrary, to the release of new educational vigour. International information on the subject of creative educational experiments is difficult as these reports may constitute open criticism of certain educational structures (both private and public): sometimes highly discriminatory, and on other occasions very tedious and sometimes simply useless.

(8) *Worldwide and Local Problems*

The educational authorities cannot escape either the worldwide or the local problems of society. North-South, East-West relations and conflicts as well as the conservatism converging on the industrial societies (sometimes Western, sometimes Eastern) exert a great deal of influence on educational systems, and this must be taken into consideration. Educators and educational programmers must fight for the best educative content if they wish reforms. It means fitting migrants into the system, fighting racism and developing the creative side of education, etc. It is true that during the last few years education has greatly expanded, but it has not made much progress from the point of view of social and international standards.

A good way to measure educational efficiency would be to identify and to make use of the above-mentioned indications for estimating educational impact on the improvement of the relationship between countries and the regard for man's individual and common rights.

The insignificant and modest multiplier effects of these educational projects are often largely due to the fact that they are frequently purely educational projects, unrelated to the problems of our societies. Politics, philosophy, economics, education, hence reflection and action, are being more and more neglected in the educational movement. Technological development is, unfortunately, considered an alternative to political, philosophical, economical and cultural activity.

III. Possible and 'Impossible' Alternatives

(1) *Basic Education*

Basic education for children, young people and adults is usually minimal. But a minimal education cannot be compared to the minimal numbers of calories necessary for survival. If it is considered desirable to make basic education available to all it must be fully standardised itself and at the same time form the beginning of a series of adjustments. Consequently, basic education cannot exist parallel to an educational system that sets rigid rules for knowledge and research. On analysing educational activities in different countries, one notices that the relationship between basic education and education as a whole is failing and often non-existent, and that the subject matter of this education is mainly directed towards adaptation and primary manual labour qualifications. Basic education has little relationship to research and development centres in the various educational fields. As for the educators, the institutionalisation of educational activities which addresses itself to a small sector of a public composed of different denominations, has possibly created jobs for certain staffs of these activities, but the working conditions of the educators in this sphere often remain uncertain and their chances of establishing a career lie frequently elsewhere. This is the explanation for so many changes of staff, resulting in fluctuation of activities. Thus basic education for children, young people and adults should be fitted directly into an educational system for all, by all.

(2) *Educational Research*

The preliminary to any educational enterprise is a careful analysis of all discourse on education and permanent research of emerging facts which could be of significance. Deeper investigation of educational discourse impedes an easy dismissal of progressive educational ideas by the forces against it: during the last few decades it has been shown how some of the educational concepts and practices could be retrieved and manipulated. Educational decentralisation and participation, lifelong education, deschooling, democratisation of education, self-training via public assistance and adult education are some of the examples.

Permanent research must continue in order to remain acquainted with the facts that emerge. All too often political decisions, educational reforms and the creation of new systems have failed owing to lack of harmony. On the other hand, whole national social sectors, both productive and educational, have been confronted with non-development due to absence of educational strategy.

(3) *Educational Administration*

Everyone agrees that different legal and administrative systems in education are necessary in order to attain various improvement programmes, but in most countries it is evident that the gap is widening between those in charge of educational activities and those in the administrative sector. The prototype presented by local and national educational institutions is often exactly the opposite to that which was proposed during the set-up when efficient productive and administrative systems were discussed. Educational administration is a fundamental element of dispute closely entwined with the repercussions it has upon educational policy and activities. It is not an easy undertaking to create and accept educational structures competent to meet new requirements, but future educational systems cannot help being a combination of stable structures in a permanent state of development.

(4) *The Challenge Ahead*

What is required is meticulous precision in research and scrutiny in the choice of educational material. Unfortunately, however, the power of rhetoric, the wink of an eye (and of an eye that is often short-sighted), concessions and the evasion of problems are not unusual, especially in the case of those responsible for the policy, activities and information concerning education. The struggles for closer investigation, clarity, and creative ideas as opposed to the manoeuvring that goes on in educational matters could avoid the application of useless, worthless and even regressive educational policies and activities. An education expanding in a multitude of ways and places, in which self-education and institutional education are already meeting or are able to meet each other, is going to require a fertile imagination in defining educational policy and adapting the existing systems; the response is often simply quantitative, with the accent more on growth than modernisation. The right to work, the right to education, free-thinking and individual opinions, the right to community life, the right to a time away from work free from self-estrangement and from the threat of being moved; these are all plans with obvious implications for education, a new challenge for reformers. The re-organisation of the objectives of production and consumption, the creation of jobs and the struggles against racism could also provide a common goal for a great many reformers — north, south, east and west.

(5) *Education For All and By All*

Education for all and by all is the condition for re-altering contemporary societies and, in the long run, the answer to a demand for basic education. This education for all and by all will be achieved and contribute to:

(a)   the recognition of individuals and countries in new cultural identities;
(b)   better relationships among countries;
(c)   the recognition of a communal world responsibility;
(d)   the realisation that only the complete and intelligent use of all human resources will allow the peaceful management and self-management of our societies.

Notes

1. UNESCO, *A summary statistical review of education in the world* (1960-82), Paris, 1984
2. OIT, 'Reprise économique et emploi', *Bulletin d'information* OIT, vol. xix, no. 3, August 1983

11 INTERCULTURAL CO-OPERATION IN HIGHER EDUCATION

Major changes in international relations and in productive systems can be forecast for the end of this century and for the twenty-first century. Intercultural co-operation through higher education could play a major role in the understanding of these changes; but today, in most countries, higher education does not very often seek to analyse and interpret contemporary and emerging human needs. Frequently, higher education activities with respect to other cultures are completely separate from mainstream academic activities. Little research has been developed to gain a better understanding of already emerging or predicted intercultural relationships, and, in addition, training activities for intercultural co-operation are limited.

Intercultural activities could give new confidence to both students and teachers in higher education, but today both are often depressed and lack vision. Building up an international society today calls for the proper evalution of human resources, but these are not always recognised in many countries of the world. Intercultural co-operation among higher education institutions should also make possible both research and practical activities — impossible in a purely national framework — by increasing access to more recent scientific findings and to human and material resources. Even within a particular society, intercultural activities also provide an opportunity for higher education institutions which are already oriented towards the outside world to become involved. In fact there exists intercultural co-operation not only among different countries but even within individual countries. However, rigid social stratification, social discrimination, and bias against minority groups can make cultural communication within a particular country most difficult.

Intercultural co-operation can help teachers and students to overcome a purely corporatist defence of their present situation and their future profession. New societal goals at the national and international levels can lead to higher educational reforms beyond the self-interest motivation. Today, reforms in higher education seem quite irrelevant to the general public, because emerging societal goals seem to be insufficiently related to these reforms and, as a result, teachers and students find themselves isolated from the wider society when their debates are limited to narrow educational reforms.

International higher education policies are becoming a part of the international power game. The ever increasing role of knowledge and of the diffusion of technology and training affect higher educational systems, and this can mean new significance for higher education of both central and marginal countries. But the dominating-dominated relationship could be aggravated as a result of developments in higher education since the more powerful countries could chose to maintain their monopoly over technological and scientific resources, and refrain from providing the requisite technologies needed in the peripheral countries.

An unbalanced intercultural co-operation is now developing in so far as marginal countries are becoming more dependent in education for: (a) hardware and software, (b) teachers in some special fields, (c) training at the post-graduate level. Peripheral countries are not in a position to refuse the present 'unbalanced co-operation'; but they can minimise the present and possible future inbalance by working towards their own cultural development. Moreover, in a number of peripheral countries, higher education is growing rapidly, but often along contradictory lines: limitations on the actual job performance, the brain drain, dependence on external validation.

The spread of training is becoming one of the most important aspects of intercultural co-operation. Sometimes centre countries refuse to provide much-needed technologies, and even when they do, it might occasionally be considered a failure. These failures can be attributed to the lack of interest by powerful firms of centre countries in the training of workers in the marginal countries in the understanding, management and control of exported technology; such exports can thus create a new type of imperialism and dependency on foreign experts. This contradiction can be overcome if the rules of the game can be unambiguously stated. Are these imports of technology useful for reinforcing the scientific and technological capacity of a country or, on the contrary, do they increase the dependence of the receiver country?[1] The cost of these imports to the receiving countries is increasing significantly, but in many cases these countries and their people have no choice but to accept the contents and the training that is provided for them.

Inequalities between the higher educational systems of different countries are increasing: in industrialised countries, higher educational development is becoming a double indicator of a new kind of consumption, and of greater popular access to some form of higher education. This expansion of higher education in the industrialised countries does not necessarily mean more international educational democracy, but it can help the marginal countries; indeed, the latter have to fight for a new educational order that involves more than mere quantitative expansion. Marginal countries have to protect themselves from dependency and from propaganda and manipulation, but simultaneously they have to profit to the maximum from the scientific and technological research done in the heavily industrialised countries. The results of human creativity and scientific research and the newly emerging industrial culture[2] belong to mankind and not just to the industrialised countries, Eastern or Western. From historical analysis we can affirm that the means and people necessary for appropriate research can come from the peripheral countries. Yet we also have to remember that Egyptian priests and Greek philosophers were not the only ones who profited from slave labour, even in our modern times, powerful economic and political elites are able to develop research because of the varied forms of exploitation within and outside their own countries.

Intercultural Co-operation and Cultural Identity

I do not think that to choose both of these is always a contradictory choice: they are compatible in situations where intercultural co-operation is not an instrument for domination. It is true that there is much ambiguity when we speak about intercultural and multicultural co-operation. In fact, empires have always been multicultural societies, in which different ethnic groups may have been accorded the same legal status. Even so, they have rarely enjoyed equal cultural, economic and social status.

Intercultural and multicultural policies which call for the dependency of given groups become a threat to cultural identity. In contemporary North-South/Centre-Periphery relationships, the international division of labour, mass media dependency, and intercultural co-operation can together become either an instrument maintaining domination, or for the creation of a new equilibrium. It is an objective fact that national and international organisations dealing with intercultural co-operation reflect both these contradictory factors.

Higher education is no longer an ivory tower: on the one hand, in all countries (free market or planned economies), the state and industry jointly, or separately, are becoming increasingly interested in higher educational policies; on the other hand, the growing relevance of foreign relationships, especially in the economic field, also mean for higher education a parallel involvement in the foreign relations of various countries.

Is it really possible through higher education to create the dependency of one nation upon another? Teachers, content, teaching technology coming from outside can increase the dependency of the marginal country; at the same time, the opening up of higher education to foreign students in the culturally advanced countries can, if it has little regard for their cultures, also bring about a new form of domination. Sometimes students and teachers in higher educational institutes in dependent marginal countries can easily find excuses for accepting restriction placed upon them concerning (a) the relevance of their research and training for their own country, and (b) their need for intellectual freedom and their potential for creativity. A dependent system of higher education results from externally determined curricular contents, methods, topics of research, means and criteria of evaluation and orientations toward the future. A dependent system of higher education contributes both to the creation of an upper oriented class towards outside cultural, intellectual and economic influences in the peripheral countries, as well as to the migration of the most talented individuals from them to the industrial countries.

How is it possible, then, to reach a new equilibrium through intercultural co-operation in higher education? First, through negotiated co-operation on a regional basis among higher educational institutions aimed at strengthening the educational capacities of higher education within participating countries. Secondly, through greater attention to migrant cultures by higher educational institutions in order to achieve a better understanding of these external cultures. Thirdly, through co-operation among national and foreign teachers in order to help students become more aware of and sensitive to different cultures. Fourthly, through the revision of academic curricula to enable foreign students to keep in touch with their own cultures whilst pursuing their studies at higher level of education. Fifthly, and most importantly, through greater intercultural co-operation for the more equal sharing of educational resources and opportunities.

From Moral Declarations to Practical Activities

How is it possible to convince the more powerful countries to take practical steps instead of merely making statements of goodwill about intercultural co-operation? In the short run, the powerful countries of East and West can develop further, while at the same time exploitation and violence continue in the Third World. But from a long-term perspective, it is to their benefit to work towards more equal co-operation among these different countries and to discover new means of achieving mutual understanding. Positive relationships between cultures and peoples are not a purely moral option, they are a necessity; as it is through political struggle tied to their mutual economic interests that people develop.

On the one hand, ideals are propounded in an effort to convince others of the utility of intercultural co-operation within higher education; on the other, the internationalisation of production and commerce have momentous consequences for education, and make intercultural co-operation a necessity in higher education. It is becoming difficult for producers and businessmen to avoid being concerned, informed, and aware of the outside cultures because markets are becoming worldwide, and education and culture play important roles in worldwide economic dynamics. Recognition of the objective necessity of intercultural co-operation is possibly the real starting point for more relevant intercultural programmes in institutions of higher education.

Juridical and Economic Aspects

Intercultural activities in higher education have to be studied carefully because the participation of foreign students in the national systems of education creates problems and obstacles. It seems, today, that in countries with positive international relations it is possible for immigrants to work in most of the productive sectors. But higher education administration has much more trouble in accommodating people from abroad than does the productive system, because evaluation procedures are less efficient and, with very few exceptions, exclude people from outside the national system.

There is not just formal higher education, but also non-formal higher education, even if the latter is not well known to most people. In fact, intercultural co-operation is developed sometimes through non-formal higher education, such as educational foundations, business schools, social events, military groups, political party organisations. We need research in this area to find out the ways in which the leading social classes of many marginal countries are made dependent. The international division of labour, and the monetary policies that are affecting the labour markets of both the Third World and the industrial countries, are also transforming the social structure of society; new class cultures are emerging and cutting across the traditional upper, middle and working-class divisions.

There also exists a non-formal higher education for people who do not have access to formal higher education, but who are quite capable, through individual and collective self-education, of acquiring skills and developing sophisticated cultures.

The limited concern of higher educational institutions for the inter-relationship of popular culture and education makes it quite difficult for them to understand non-formal programmes of education both in other countries and in low-status social groups. Knowledge of different non-formal programmes can lead to a deeper understanding of the different forms of communication: oral, visual and non-verbal. An understanding of these forms of communication is indeed poor in many academic circles. Frequently, oral traditions are ignored in the inter-cultural relationship between countries.[3]

What does intercultural co-operation in education and, specifically, in higher education, mean for the marginal people of the industrialised countries and for the great majority of people in the peripheral countries? How is it possible to encourage all people, including migrant workers, refugees, minority groups and the least privileged people of the various countries[4] to participate in the planning and the definition of policies and programmes for the promotion of intercultural co-operation? A first evaluation of contemporary intercultural activities in higher education indicates that, for the present, these people do not have the opportunity to contribute to the formulation of higher educational policies, for among them very few are consumers of higher education.

Neither the mass media and the communication infrastructures in general, nor the emigration of the intelligentsia help peripheral countries to develop original thinking in the realm of higher education. Often in these countries, creative individuals are productive in this area, but their ideas circulate only through the people and may only by chance reach official government circles in their own countries.

Mass media, resource centres and libraries in universities collect documents that are produced and distributed through routine channels; this means that alternative and critical cultural productive work does not reach them. Intercultural co-operation requires vigorous action by individuals involved in the mass media, archivists and librarians, in collecting as much information as possible, using every possible means — cassette recordings, the translations of documents written in local languages, the collection of documents other than only those already in writing, the stimulation of contributions from countries considered marginal as far as written production is concerned, and so on.

If education were orientated more towards production, research and creativity, it would be easier for the responsible people in education to communicate with each other. Production and research would have more compatible languages as they would both deal with similar problems. Two important dimensions of education are often neglected in higher education: the creative production of knowledge and the possibility of the transformation of the 'reciprocal relations between different age spans and age groups' for the development of greater involvement by these participatory groups.[5] The achievement of these two functions can contribute positively to intercultural co-operation; while prejudices, racism, intellectual dominance, etc. are often associated with a purely passive cultural attitude.

Present-day problems connected with intercultural co-operation (migrants, refugees, employment, racism, etc.) are those of both young and adult people, who are faced with a complex and changing world; the search for solutions to emerging needs should thus be one of the primary goals of higher education. The acquisition of knowledge is becoming one of the most appropriate productive activities for many countries during the process of industrialisation and post-industrialisation.

In the meantime higher education, as a major institution for the production of knowledge, is facing a crisis the world over since it is possible that the acquisition and production of knowledge may be moving away from the higher educational institutions. This question has to be taken seriously. A monopoly on the development of knowledge by higher education and research institutions is certainly not what is needed today, but these institutions do have a more important role to play in the development of knowledge than they exercise at present.

New curricula for higher education are needed to prepare people to cope with such problems as those related to: the management of national and international societies in a future unified world;[6] the ecology of the whole environment, i.e. sky, water, earth; international migration; and the internationalisation of economic and financial markets. Production and finance are becoming international, but public, national and international institutions are too weak to deal adequately with the problems resulting from the internationalisation of production. Few studies are made, because few institutions or states believe themselves to be directly concerned.

Solutions to ecological problems cannot be restricted to the national level. Existing international organisations have tried to develop research and to give some guidelines concerning these problems. But can we ask who is to implement the policies formulated?

It is not the facts of international and regional migration but the current dimensions that are new. Migrant workers are often poorly assisted at the regional level, and often at the national level they have no kind of assistance or protection.

Although international cultural relationships and life itself are full of moral platitudes, little research exists to lend support to concrete action. In this sense, higher education has the role of building the necessary store of knowledge for the construction of effective instruments to improve international and intercultural relationships.

How are these problems studied? New curricula are needed, but, equally, the traditional ones have to be rethought. All programmes and their contents have to be redirected towards achieving a wider international intercultural perspective. Reforms in universities and higher educational institutions should not be limited to the development of special departments for the study of international and intercultural relationships. These departments might give the impression, falsely, that they are sufficient for taking care of intercultural co-operation, and that the contribution of other departments is not necessary. Moreover, when these departments are too separate, they can easily be manipulated and controlled by different ministers to ensure that they can, by the selective provision of funds, curtail the scope of the foreign affairs areas researched. They can support covert government activities in the same way.

As higher education is becoming more important in international relations, it follows that the more powerful countries have a special interest in controlling the educational policies of higher educational institutions, in their own as well as in other countries. In this respect, it is easier to manipulate just one department than the entire higher educational system.

Intercultural co-operation in higher education is often ambiguous, contradictory and repressive. Nevertheless, it is full of promise. The achievement of international co-operation is a difficult task, and one difficulty arises from the fact that, frequently, those chosen to represent the various countries are not the best people. If higher educational institutions and teachers are not knowledgeable enough about their own countries, they can formulate and implement projects that have serious negative implications for them. If those responsible for educational planning accept the contributions of foreign specialists without possessing the necessary information concerning the cultural orientations of these specialists, they can inadvertently select people whose aims are opposite to their own.

International academic networks are organised in such a way that some countries, with or without any scientific primacy, are allowed to lead in a given field. 'Top people' in peripheral countries are therefore obliged, and in some cases even 'choose' to accept external international leadership. Wide gaps between the level of scientific achievements of different countries exist; to ignore them is counterproductive. This, however, does not imply that scientific networks will necessarily involve relations of dependence: the creation of a network results from a political act in which the use of academic violence is accepted or rejected as an option.

A major obstacle to intercultural development in higher education is the very ignorance of the most 'cultivated people' themselves. Teachers, often very competent in their own subjects, sometimes ignore international realities and cultures that are not local nor national. Racism (open, hidden or unconscious – the latter is the most widespread form); the rigidities of educational structures that make for difficulties in accommodating people coming from other countries and other educational systems; a declining mobility even within national higher educational systems (more and more students graduate from the universities where they will later teach) – these are some of the reasons for this ignorance at the highest levels.

Poor intercultural co-operation among formal higher educational institutions is an indicator of the cultural poverty of these institutions; technological and scientific achievements do not alone reflect full cultural development.

Modern cultural co-operation can profit from a broader and more universal knowledge of the history of different societies. Wealthy countries usually know little about the historical traditions of the more marginal countries. If we want equal and democratic intercultural co-operation, it is necessary to foster historical research at national and international levels; it is not possible to conceive of creative intercultural co-operation without first an equal respect for different cultural identities.

Intercultural research and production require a long-term commitment and active support; but the higher education timetables in many countries still consider these activities as more or less marginal, and even as little more than a leisure-time activity for the summer vacation. But, if we believe that the understanding of the intercultural dimension is emerging as one of the conditions for the survival of higher education, then we have to put intercultural activities among the priorities for higher educational programmes.

Real projects concerning individual and collective human rights, strategies for peace, development, etc. cannot be merely episodes for higher education institutions. On the contrary, they are among the most relevant activities of their programmes, and a starting point for higher education research and training activities.

As far as practical structural solutions are concerned, it is possible to envisage (a) intercultural teaching units in universities at regional and international levels where national and foreign teachers can contribute to the international curriculum;[7] (b) common schemes of validation to allow easy transfer of students and teachers from one institution to another either within the region or at international level; (c) formal and non-formal training and self-directed learning programmes that enable teachers and students to become acquainted with historical, contemporary and future realities of different societies; (d) more collective self-management (if teachers are awaiting new directions from higher channels, it will be difficult to meet the demands emerging for intercultural co-operation).

Progressive teachers in the industrial countries often feel frustrated because they consider themselves marginal and powerless. They sometimes try to find meaning to their lives by pursuing personal comfort, alternative lifestyles and even by adopting alternative world views acceptable within the marginal countries, but often associated with minority or revolutionary movements within their own. They could play an important role because, being at the very centre of the world of knowledge they have access to relevant information with which they can fight oppression both within their own and other countries, and give support to those who are struggling in countries where repression is widespread. They need to improve their communication with under-privileged individuals and groups of both Northern and Southern countries, and they can be active in finding the right channels of communication and in working for the resolution of real problems. The feeling of hopelessness and exasperation will probably disappear once they begin to act.

An example of such a problem that requires co-operation in higher education is the search for an alternative to the arms race. To develop intercultural co-operation means, in a sense, to fighting the arms race, and this includes all countries, East and West. This is not enough, but a better understanding among people can contribute to strengthening people struggling to convert a war-prone society into a peaceful society. The following proposals, originally made to trade unionists, could also be directed towards higher education institutions:

First, to discover the technical practicalities of converting arms-production into the production of useful goods for non-military purposes, and to identify such socially useful alternatives for existing production facilities.

Second, to identify social needs in developed countries and similar development needs in underdeveloped countries to which converted arms industries could be applied.

Third, to examine ways of financing, through central and local government and in other ways, a major increase in non-military production that would be acceptable to the great majority of people to the same extent that defence budgets are now acceptable.

Fourth, to prepare teaching materials on this subject, including plans and case studies, that could be used in many different forms of adult education, where the question of arms-conversion could properly be raised . . . [8]

Intercultural co-operation at the international level in higher education itself reflects the tendencies within higher education. Higher education, open to all irrespective of age, and type of talent, at local and national levels, creates a positive environment for intercultural co-operation. Higher education, orientated to lifelong education, cannot be satisfied with education restricted to one age group, or to one social class, or to the ideology of a single political party, or again to a purely nationalist outlook, which is antagonistic to international co-operation. Intercultural co-operation cannot be but dialectical, and inventive, free of artificial barriers and dogmas.

A critical analysis of international co-operation in higher education is urgently needed. As a matter of fact, on one side there is a lack of this necessary co-operation, on the other, there is an abundance of false intercultural activities, which conceal racism, offer an irrelevant perspective, new colonial manipulation, separation of the elite from the people, the arbitrary selection of only one part of the culture (i.e. an incorrect interpretation of folklore), brain drain, etc. In addition, a critical analysis of the possible future trends of higher education would also be useful since the views often put forward today of its future are often inadequate; demography and scientific development are taken in consideration, but not the other emerging problems of mankind, nor the interrelationship between countries.

As we have said before, education is bound to be strongly affected by the changing patterns of the world of work as well as by the new relationships that will emerge between 'northern' and 'southern' countries. These problems will become central for university teachers and students alike, if higher education is to remain central to cultural life in the future.

A working dialogue should now begin between progressive, scientifically oriented and creative people of higher educational institutions throughout the world. Censorship, manipulation through ideology, and social and intellectual conformism are the worst enemies of intercultural co-operation.

Notes

1. L.C. Pasinetti, *Structural Changes and Economic Growth*, Cambridge, UK, University Press, 1981
2. M. Dia, *Islam, Sociétés africaines et culture industrielle*, Dakar, Les nouvelles éditions africaines, 1975, p. 126
3. A. Flugerang, *About Understanding, Ideas and Observations on Cross-cultural Communication*, Upsala, Dag Hammarskjöld Foundation, 1982
4. J.C. Tedesco, *Reproductivismo educativo y sectores populares en América latina*, Caracas, Clacso, 1983, p. 39
5. F. Mahler, *Introducere in juventologie*, Bucarest, Editura Stintifica si Enciclopedica, 1983, p. 294
6. S.C. Dube, *Development Perspectives for the 1980s*, New Delhi, Abhinav/UN, 1983
7. Conversation with I. Dandolo, Paris, 1983
8. M. Barrat Brown, *Arms Industry Conversion. An Adult and Research Project*, London, Bertrand Russell Peace Foundation, 1983

12 THE HUMAN SCIENCES AND NORTH-SOUTH RELATIONS

Could the human sciences have a part to play in bringing about peace? Or on the contrary, might they not reinforce conflicts between countries? Ignorance of the history and current problems of different countries creates or increases prejudice and racism, which are one source of direct and indirect violence. To emphasise this aspect is not to ignore the economic, social and political factors which also engender prejudice and racism. Unfortunately, a review of the results of research in the area of the human sciences suggests that, up to now, these sciences have often contributed to the reinforcement of cultural dependency of Third World countries, and have been a means of conveying prejudice against them.

North-South relations are today an important theme of economic and political debate. But do the peoples of the North know enough about the living conditions, aspirations and cultures of the great majority of the peoples of the South (and also, moreover, about their own most marginalised groups)? In the North, particularly, the handling of research conducted for and in Third World countries, and the insensitivity of researchers towards the developing problems of remote countries, are inadequate as sources of information; in the South, the dependency often present in economic and political life conditions research (this dependency is, moreover, reinforced by the social science research which often incorporates the interests, values and objects of the countries of the North).

The feeling of powerlessness on the part of researchers and, in general, of intellectuals oriented to North-South politics, has been the source in certain circumstances of wholly ideological and dogmatic analyses of North-South relations, analyses which do not contribute much to our knowledge of the dynamic and contradictory realities of Third World countries and their international relations.

The powerlessness of many researchers leads them into a voluntarist language:

> The voluntarist language of the 'integrity' of research, of the 'integrity' of the researcher, and of the 'integrity' of the contents of research conceals the essential problem: the need of professional

academics to problematise their practice and transform it into research which is precise, concrete, contemporary and creative.[1]

But what are the disciplines that could be considered to be human sciences: sociology, psychology, history, economics, pedagogy, political science — perhaps even poetry?[7] This last — if one could call poetry a science — is perhaps one of the most powerful forms of communication between cultures. At a meeting of scientists (exact sciences, natural and human) one often feels the threads of dependency running from the North to the South; by contrast, at a meeting of poets communication is much more two-way, everyone being eager to learn about the discoveries and the expression of others and not to instruct them.

When it comes to knowledge in the countries of the North, there are two categories: those countries whose knowledge of the South is by way of colonialism, and those which know the South in the post- or neo-colonial period. While during the colonial period the most significant sources of knowledge can be found in documents referring to economic and military relations and cultural and ideological action, today the most significant and the most revealing — often in their brutality — can be discovered by studying the economic, military, cultural and ideological facts.

The development of the human sciences on the basis of equality between countries could be an important aspect of cultural co-operation at the international level, but until now, when it comes to the formal human sciences (fortunately, the 'non-formal' human sciences are developing independently), subordination has been strongly reinforced through the financing of research, through the training of researchers and through the imposition of the values of the North into these sciences.

The institutionalisation of research into North-South relations by means of bilateral and international co-operation, has not so far contributed much to the reciprocal knowledge of North and South. Those countries who wish to maintain unchanged the relations between North and South (of dependency for some and domination for the others) have so far withheld their co-operation.

Influenced at the same time by the need of industrialised countries to develop new markets and by the appalling living conditions of many of the peoples of the world, bilateral and international co-operation has developed to bring economic 'aid' to deprived countries. The human sciences are involved in this process, but unfortunately often only to reinforce prevailing ideologies and politics: not only are the 'auxiliary' human sciences of co-operation and aid not used for the benefit of countries receiving 'aid and co-operation', but they have influenced and make dependent both the researchers and the objective of the human sciences in the countries of the South.

Relations between the human sciences and development programmes are rather curious:

> social sciences have been most often employed after the experiences of development have been set in train, that is to say in order to 'accompany' them, in order to study after the event the effects upon the people concerned. Such a use of social sciences is precisely contrary to what ought to happen.[2]

Faced with the ambiguity and compromise of various non-endogenous development programmes there are likewise two other kinds of reaction: return to the traditional cultural inheritance, or refusal to engage in the politics of development.

Between the choice of compromise or that of refusal — seen now as national interdependence — the response of human sciences researchers in the countries of the North and the South is perhaps to get more involved with the people and with observation of the reality of the situation. Human sciences based upon methodological perfectionism and least concerned with reality have little to fear from power; on the other hand, rigorous analysis and strategies for action, the *raison d'être* of human sciences, meet with the most determined obstruction.

To free the human sciences of their colonialist, dogmatic and class-based traditions, in the West and in the East, is not an easy task, especially at a time when racism and dogmatism are as strong as ever. To free also the language of colonialist traditions is one of the tasks of the human sciences responsible for having contributed to the development of that language: 'The word tribalism is only used for the Africans and the Indians. Why? Scientific explanations of the term have been put forward. For me, it evokes the herd, pure and simple.'[3]

The resurgence of racism, the feeling of superiority of some over others, and the direct and indirect violence which flows from it, could be reflected by those human sciences which have contributed so little to exposing the absurdity of racism and the feelings of superiority of certain countries. For example, facts about the economic relations between countries provide evidence that, in general, all countries profit from those countries which are poor and dependent, and the most industrialised countries profit most, contrary to the widespread claim to the effect that these countries make political sacrifices by their guarantees of aid, by welcoming migrant workers, by buying at good prices raw materials or foodstuffs from the countries of the Third World.

Independent development of the human sciences and the focus upon the problems of different societies: the choice is made by many researchers.

> Indigenization does not involve a retreat of the social sciences into national shells. It is aimed principally at a redefinition of focus and at purposive efforts to develop dynamic perspectives on national problems and critical issues of public policy.[4]

The indigenisation of the social sciences, and of the human sciences in general, would at last make possible relations on an equitable basis between the various researchers: 'In reality, what had happened was the emergence and acceptance of a patron-client relationship between the social scientists of the more affluent countries and their counterparts in the less developed countries.'[5]

Analysis of the national perspective can nevertheless include, or exclude, the problems of ethnic minorities (or even majorities) which are, or have been, oppressed. The social sciences could make an important contribution towards restoring cultural identity in helping to recover the

> four fundamental elements of the social consciousness of nations: (1) Recovery of the homeland: historic territory, actual territory, settlement, ecosystems, etc. . . (2) recovery of past time, which is to say restoring national history as an objective and analytic unity in the regional and national context . . . (3) Recovery of national ideas and beliefs, which is to say the 'rediscovery' of different nationalities, systems of belief and classification, of the essential characteristic of the national language . . . (4) Exploration of the future, which is to say investigation of and speculation upon social planning for the people by the leaders of the nation . . . [6]

The indigenisation of research does not signify complete self-sufficiency, but the establishment of guidelines to permit research which is of significance for every country:

> at the present time, an increasing number of developing countries

believe that the foreign researchers whom they welcome should take into account their needs and their possibilities; they consider furthermore that their research should be conducted in collaboration with the specialists of the host country and that the results should be as much available to the one as to the other.[7]

The most prestigious political leaders of the Third World, unfortunately often isolated by their power, have been more interested in a culture which reflects contemporary issues without discriminating between the countries of the South and the countries of the North:

> For a culture which ignores reality is a culture condemned to ineffectiveness and oblivion, a culture without perspective, decadent, concealing its own lifelessness. On the basis of such a sketch it is possible to discern the aspect of tomorrow's industrial culture, which will be a culture of everyone and which will be the work of everyone . . . addressing itself to everyone, its language will be accessible to all, even to people of an oral culture. Its mysteries will not be reserved to the circle of the initiated, the technical dramatists, nor to the privileged groups who appropriate to themselves the power as well as the knowledge.[8]

The human sciences which could respond to the problems of the countries of the South require a significant output of literature concerned with those countries and in the language of those countries. The absence of such texts, and thus the dependence upon external sources, has been one of the factors making for the dependency of the human sciences in most of the countries of the South.[9]

The increasing cost and sophistication of research could become a further cause for the dependency of the human sciences in the societies of the South and for neo-colonialisation by means of these sciences. Indigenisation could also be achieved through research centred on the fundamental problems of these societies and at a much reduced cost.

The research programme of the Centre for Studies in African Development (CEDA) in Upper Volta is a response to the need to focus research upon the specific problems of the country:

> The CEDA is a centre based in Africa and exclusively devoted to studying the African system(s) of production and reproduction in its dynamic whole with a view to constructing a theoretical model

of progress in our societies. Its concern is therefore with action-research: but with research entirely rooted in our contexts, with a view to evolving a global theory in relation to political practice and cultural identity, central concerns which are frequently neglected.[10]

The development of the human sciences also requires increasing resources not only for research but also for publication and training; by these means the dependency of the countries of the South is often reinforced. The response to this dependency on the part of scientists and the people could occur on at least two levels: on the one hand by increasing the rigour and independence of research, publication and training, on the other hand (when human sciences are developed in dependent institutional settings — although the nature and contradictions of this dependence must nevertheless be carefully analysed) by constantly denouncing the subtle or the more obvious manipulation of the human sciences.

It is also important to establish more balanced relations between the various human sciences. For example, between the political creativity of 1968 and the more sombre economic determinism of 1983, it would be necessary to grasp economics in a context of cultural forces of resistance, creativity and production. The only economic discourse, in so far as it is a purely technical discourse, is an attack by the North upon the South to deny hope and justification to struggle and resistance.

The difficulties of developing the human sciences in the Third World countries (often manipulated or absolutely suppressed) have implications for the training of their peoples and especially for their ruling classes. The contribution of the social sciences to the training of the ruling classes is evident: hence the interest of the most powerful countries in training their own elites by making available all the uncensored facts, even those which do not correspond to the ideologies of those elites. On the other hand, in the countries of the South, often censorship of the human sciences (in research and training) is brought to bear upon the training of elites, especially that part of it which concerns the situation of their own countries.

The impression that the North and the South are both subject to the laws of economics and, at the same time, that they could to some extent transcend them, could make human sciences researchers conscious that their preoccupations are perhaps common ones:

historical necessity, which for the critic of political economy coincides with the 'worldwide' role of the conductor and determinant of market-forces (and with their 'contradictions') suggests that it may be possible to subdue history as much as nature merely by complying with its laws. These observations could lead to a provisional conclusion, and in some way help to escape from the dilemma, in the words of Wittgenstein: 'We could invent natural history itself'.[11]

A permanent construction of the human sciences, with contributions from everyone, and not their imposition by the North upon the South, could be extraordinarily rich in its contents and new cultural perspectives. So many issues fundamental to the future of our societies could at last be identified, studied and better understood in response to real and urgent problems.

At the outset, the urgency of the human sciences in the industrialising societies of the nineteenth century was related to certain urgent problems being posed by industrialisation. Interdependent development, on the basis of equality, is amongst the most complex problems and, in effect, has been too little studied. Research into alternatives has been continually postponed or else limited to vague scenarios. The construction of an international society, multicultural and non-racist, where the rights of *individuals and* groups of men and women would be respected, would require a reformulation of the human sciences which took account of cultural traditions, conditions of life, international relations, until now hardly ever studied by the human sciences. This reformulation of the human sciences would require a new epistemology of such sciences which took account of the various social and cultural realities until now either ignored or only partially analysed by the human sciences. This new critical education would be the result of formal and, above all, 'non-formal' researchers (these latter being excluded, in many countries, or perhaps in the great majority of countries, from institutional centres of research).

The censors of *Les fleurs du mal*[12] are still with us in the human sciences — and they can be found in very many countries, and in international relations. Censorship and regulation lead unfortunately to a failure to understand the problems, unluckily, when all is said and done, for all countries. Hence the concern for the struggle for international co-operation in the human sciences, founded upon the analysis of reality.

Notes

1. H. Radetich, *La retorica de la Praxis* (Notas para el analysis del discurso sobre la investicación), Mexico, UAG, EGYL, 1982, p. 7, mimeo

2. D. de Coppet, 'Les sciences sociales et la coopération avec les pays en voie de développement' in M. Godelier, *Les sciences de l'homme et de la société en France, Rapports complémentaires*, Paris, La Documentation française, 1982, p. 96

3. S. N'Dongo, 'Situation des paysans', *Notre fleuve*, Paris, UGTSF, 1981, p. 7

4. S.C. Dube, *On Crisis and Commitment in Social Sciences*, New Delhi, Abhivav Publication, 1983, p. 73

5. Ibid., p. 68

6. S. Varese (ed.), *Etnias y lenguas en Oaxaca', Cuadernos de Trabajo*, Oaxaca, no. 1 (Mexico, Dirección general de culturas populares)

7. Zhao Fu Shu, 'Les sciences sociales et la modernisation de la Chine', *Revue internationale des sciences sociales*, no. 2, 1982, 372

8. M. Dia, *Islam, sociétés africaines et culture industrielle*, Dakar, Les nouvelles éditions africaines, 1975, p. 126

9. R. Glass, *A New Series of Teaching Material in the Social Sciences for Third World Countries*, London, Centre for Urban Studies, 1980, mimeo

10. J. Ki-Zerbo, *Le Centre d'Etudes pour le Développement africain*, Ouagadougou, CEDA, 1981

11. S. Veca, 'Economia e politica tra natura e artificio', *Prassi e teoria*, no. 6, 1980, Milano, F. Angeli, 136

12. C. Baudelaire, *Les fleurs du mal*, Paris, Poulet-Malassis, Paris, 1857

13 THE EDUCATIONAL IMPLICATIONS OF RECENT SCIENTIFIC, TECHNOLOGICAL AND CULTURAL EXCHANGES BETWEEN JAPAN AND CHINA

This chapter is based on short visits to Japan and China, readings of articles and books by Chinese, Japanese and Western writers and researchers, and many years of acquaintance with Japanese and Chinese people. It is written by a Westerner who is interested in achieving a better understanding of a region of the world's rich culture. There is no attempt to make simple judgements, for the purpose is to find new ways to understand the educational processes within and between countries.

A comparison between China and Japan should take into consideration some demographic and economic data[1] without at the same time being too deterministic:

Table 13.1: Population and GNPs of China and Japan, 1981

	Population (millions)	GNP (1,000 million US $)	GNP *per capita* US $
Japan	117.64	1,186.43	10,080
China	991.30	299.77	300

The relationship between China and Japan in the field of education has been a part of their history for many centuries. In this chapter recent trends are analysed, taking into account cultural, economic and technological exchanges. An attempt is made to look carefully at how non-educational components have influenced the educational system, and how a country can be influenced by other countries and by international reality.

Educational analysis deserves to be based on data. The categorisation of individual countries as 'developed' or 'developing' is always ambiguous. As an example, although China is considered as a developing country, its trade patterns are closer to those of industrial nations. In 1978, 52 per cent of Chinese exports were sent to developing countries; in the same year, manufactured products composed 47.5 per cent of Chinese exports, as compared, for example, with 21 per cent for Argentina.

The complexity of the relationship between China and Japan is appearing clearly to some observers:

It looks as if Japan will need China more than China will need Japan, who, for example, would like very much to have access to Chinese oil and coal. Searching for capital groups and technology for its long-term development, China has many options . . . and the Chinese are sending external signals to Japan that economics, and trade in particular, cannot be divorced from political and military issues.[2]

Indeed, a number of people in Japan are becoming aware of the risk of a purely commercial relationship between the two countries: 'If China, for example, is regarded by the Japanese simply as a supremely important market for Japanese groups and nothing else, international relations in the long run would be adversely affected'.[3]

The data in Table 13.2 concerning Japan's foreign trade should also be taken into consideration in order to study the economic relationship between China and Japan from the proper perspective:

Table 13.2: Distribution of Japanese Trade 1971-84 (1,000 million US $)[4]

	Total	With USA		With China		With USSR	
	$	$	% of total	$	% of total	$	% of total
1971	43.7	12.6	28.9	0.9	2.1	0.9	2.1
1975	104.4	22.9	21.9	3.8	3.8	2.8	2.6
1984	270.3	56.3	20.9	9.3	3.4	4.6	1.7

From Table 13.2 it may be so seen that in real terms for Japan the most relevant trade is with the USA, but since 1971 there has been a significant upturn in trade with China. The economic ties between China and Japan are relevant, particularly for China: in 1978 about 50 per cent of Chinese exports to developed market economic countries (DMECs) went to Japan, for more than US $2,000 million.[5] In 1983, China's global commercial exchange was on the order of US $10,000 million.[6] 'Sino-japanese cooperation in China's efforts to tool up its factories dates back to September 8, 1980 when the Chinese first brought up the issue.'[7]

The Chinese have 'judged it wiser to spend their limited financial resources for tooling up, modernising their existing factories first, and building a more solid foundation for industrial development before embarking on new plant imports'.[8]

Through trade, China seeks to import knowledge and skills, and not only of facilities and goods:

China has been promoting diversified trade as a means of introducing advanced facilities and technology from abroad and has been seeking Japan's cooperation. Although such conditional trade is not in itself in strict accordance with the principles of a free-trade, the Japanese side needs to take a positive approach in the interest of further promoting business with China.[9]

Importing technologies and equipments in some cases obliges one to borrow funds. The Chinese are careful in this respect. In the words of one Chinese official: 'Since China's economic mechanism has yet to be established, we have few people from abroad. Therefore, we cannot depend on foreign loans with higher interest rates.'[10]

The PRC's [People Republic of China] exports and imports will grow at an annual rate of 5 to 6 percent. This coincides with the trend of the last 25 years. If this should happen, then no important change should be expected in the PRC's dual position as a moderate borrower and moderate capital lender.[11]

China seems to be careful in borrowing because she does not want to compromise her internal and international development. She wants to remain master of her economic life.

It would be worthwhile to analyse Chinese and Japanese policies concerning international aid and the new international economic order. However, because space does not permit, suffice it to note that China now pursues a policy of extending credit to other developing nations. The new loans to the Chinese government put China in a position similar to that of industrial countries, of receiving loans and giving credit and aid to other countries. In order to continue this present policy of international aid, however, China must maintain a balance in her foreign trade. This will not be an easy task.

The richness of the history of Sino-Japanese ties makes it possible to find common trends. For example China and Japan share an attitude towards time and nature. The Chinese and Japanese consider themselves and other people from an historical perspective, and they usually try to live in harmony with nature instead of defeating her. Chinese and Japanese gardens, for example, are invariably respected, while in contrast European gardens are often violated.[12]

But there is an interesting contrast in the way that China and Japan are developing: from 'a Japanese worldview and Chinese expertise' in the nineteenth century, towards Japanese expertise and a Chinese worldview in the present decades.[13] If this observation is correct, then it is worth considering what the effects of these changes will be upon future co-operation between these two countries.

Capital and commerce are not the only objects of trade between China and Japan: culture, patterns of participation in the community and in social productive and political life, forms of mediation with the outside world, models of aid and co-operation with other countries are increasingly confronting each other with the expansion of economic and technological exchange between the two countries. In this respect China's influence on Japan needs to be carefully studied. The Chinese revolution and its repercussions (workers' participation, community involvement, students' unrest, etc.) and Chinese international policy (co-operation and aid to Third World countries) have had an impact on Japanese progressive political groups and especially on the youth of Japan. Artists have also had a significant input since the Beijing spring of 1979-80 when the Chinese artistic world creatively communicated with other national and international communities.

The crisis of family and community traditions as a result, among others, of new productive patterns, is common to both countries. There is not yet a clear understanding that new patterns of behaviour of people, and especially of youth, are closely related to changes in the organisation of work and to their impact on social structures. Education and the reinforcement of the law (as far as the death penalty is concerned) are considered to be the solution to social problems. The real answers, however, are to be found in scientific and technological developments directed towards the achievement of greater social equality.

'Know-how' or 'expertise' has become the most desirable good for China in the Chinese-Japanese exchange. These two countries are of some interest because in considering them we can evaluate the difficulties and the problems that are facing two countries with different levels of economic development. On one side we have Japan, a country that is interested in exporting capital and technology;[14] on the other side we have China, which is interested in acquiring new technologies, but at the same time is trying to pay for this input through its own production, and not just through the spending of foreign currency, i.e. through the export of raw materials.

Chinese and Japanese relations, from the perspective of the international division of labour, may be in a transition period from a vertical towards a horizontal division of labour. In this respect, the statements of a Japanese and of a Chinese scholar are revealing:

Professor Kojima Kiyoshi of Hitotsubashi University maintains that economic relations between developed and developing countries should not be those between the dominating and the dominated and advanced industrial countries . . . should cooperate to raise the economic level and industrial structure of developing countries.[15]

Although Chinese professor Ling Xing-Quang acknowledges that this is an ideal of international exchange, he maintains that the reality of the world does not bear witness to this ideal. He is still confident, however, that the present vertical division of labour will, at some point in the future, become a more horizontal one.

It is interesting to analyse the problem of selection and reproduction through an examination of the system of education within both societies. In Japan selection occurs at the very end of upper secondary education, at which point Japanese students have to pass difficult examinations to achieve the right to enter the more esteemed universities. In China, the entrance into higher education is also very competitive.[16] Although the educational systems of both countries are structured differently, the problem of selection is raised at the upper secondary level, through formal selection in China and through an intense preparation for higher education in Japanese schools. Maybe for both societies, it is relevant to see how initial training is integrated with lifelong education policies and practices that allow all Japanese and Chinese citizens to be permanently incorporated into the educational process.

In both China and Japan lifelong education is today a topic of public debate, and is promoted by both governments as an answer to the growing demand for education among young people and adults, who have left the formal educational system either voluntarily or because social pressures have forced them to do so. Both countries are also very concerned with extended higher education, as a part of these lifelong education policies. It is relevant to ask whether, in such a context, lifelong education policies merely serve to justify given systems of social selection, or whether they help to create democratic educational institutions. There is no one answer: all educational policies and practices are the outcomes of unpredictable struggles within society.

Education is becoming an instrument for the regulation of the supply and the demand of the labour force in present day China and Japan, increasingly so in the latter because of the various consequences of automation.

Analysing both supply and demand sides of the Chinese labour force situation helps to further our understanding of the phenomenon:

> Supply side factors include: population growth in general and its impact through persons in the work-age group, the rate of increase in productivity, the number of youth staying in school beyond the starting work-age, the quality of trained personnel, changes in rural-urban population proportions, the labour participation rate, etc. Demand side factors which are important include the variety and development of different types of enterprise, labour-intensive versus capital-intensive, state versus collective as part of a broad development model, the rate of economic growth and industrial development, in general and by sectors, the labour productivity rate, industrial organization policy, labour allocation system, etc.[17]

The question arises whether the effort made to improve the quality of middle schools and secondary specialised education, to upgrade key-schools (where the ratio of teachers to pupils is particularly positive), and to stress vocational education within the place of work, is leading to a dual society and towards greater inequality (social groups, urban versus rural areas, etc.).

A common approach can be found in the Chinese and the Japanese education concerning vocational education within the place of work. In both cases the relevance of productive structures in training is evident, maybe more within the Japanese system where, since the 1970s, the enterprises tend to have full responsibility for youth and adult vocational education.[18] In Chinese youth and adult workers' education, accomplishments have been substantial:

> It is reported that from 1978-81 alone over 130 million new literates have been generated and over 38 million semi-literates have been raised to primary school equivalency level . . . About one half million workers are currently enrolled in factory-run universities and in spare-time colleges sponsored by provinces and municipalities . . . [19]

The implications on society of past and present Chinese educational policies have been studied by Chinese and outside observers: 'To promote simultaneously active investment in higher education and compulsory basic instruction puts a strain on the material means available, but it also created other tensions, as some Chinese educators have pointed out'.[20]

There is in China a permanent effort to build a diversified and a flexible educational system both full-time and part-time, for there is a strong demand for more education in both the urban and rural regions. The problem is to combine flexibility and the maximum of equality as far as the different social groups are concerned. Maybe the main contradiction is not between the rural and urban areas, but within the rural areas themselves, for decentralisation has had different consequences on both the poorer and richer rural communities.

> We must set up the schools we lack and adapt measures suited to the time and local conditions. In this way, we not only can meet different needs, making up the deficiency of a single full-time study system, but also can give more people a chance to study. This will be a good way to raise the scientific and cultural level of the entire nation.[21]

The question of decentralisation is relevant to both societies. The combination of agriculture and industry still exists in contemporary Japan.

> In the case of Oita, there is the combination of local technology with advanced technology. This combination comprises two types. The first is the result of an initiative taken by local industries and the local administrative authorities; the second results from the co-ordination between agriculture and industry which leads to a structural organisation by which each locality specialises in the production of a given product, thus creating specialisation by village or by city or by product.[22]

Oita is an example of an advanced post-industrial city; but even so, questions concerning the relationship between local and advanced technology (but are the two mutually antagonistic?) and between agriculture and industry are still of considerable relevance.

Not only today but since the very first years of the Chinese revolution, Japan has been studied by the Chinese. Japan's industrial revolution influenced Chinese political leaders; the success in Japanese agriculture and its consequences on both light and heavy industries continue to be carefully analysed by Chinese leaders. But at the same time, as Y.Z. Luo has noted, the concern for self-reliance is always there:

In the introduction of new technology from foreign countries, there is both the problem of not paying attention to the introduction of such technology for a long time, and the phenomenon of disregarding our own scientific and technological capabilities while blindly introducing things from the outside.[23]

In China the effort to achieve technological development has alternated between more centralised and more decentralised patterns of development. As one observer noted:

The systemic propensity to multiply smokestack industries based on currently available technology and the difficulty the centrally planned system experiences in sensing the direction of technological progress, are compounded by the left's preference for oxcart and bicycle-type technology, its obsession with self-reliance, anti-intellectualism, and utopianism.[24]

More recently, steps have been taken towards greater decentralisation. Some of the new policies concern questions of technological innovation:

Innovation and diffusion activities are to be focused on agriculture problems and techniques and on upgrading the technical base of light consumer industries, as well as in cultural production, through reducing energy and raw material costs.[25]

A more decentralised pattern of investment has also been pursued.[26] Although 'Local fiscal autonomy has led to an excessive dispersion of funds',[27] the new decentralised co-operative management scheme seems to be efficient as well as innovative in so far as the creation of joint-venture-type operations is concerned.

Some data concerning Chinese consumption indicate that decentralisation has achieved some results.

The fact that the increase in *per capita* consumption in the past four years has occurred largely in the countryside is strong evidence of the success of the distribution system in moving commodities not to areas of effective monetary demand, but to areas of effective political demand. Had the cash income increases realized by peasants not been transformable into consumption increases the incomes policy would have been ineffective. The policy has been successful in redistributing income to rural residents while protecting the real income of urban residents. However the redistribution has not been without cost, (inflation, among others) and the principal manifestations of that cost are found in the state budget.[28]

The past history of China and Japan, as far as decentralisation is concerned, should not be forgotten:

Comparing China and Japan we see that the problem was not that China was too bureaucratic but that China was not bureaucratic enough. Japan became a modern bureaucratic national state; China became increasingly decentralized as it was incorporated into the world economy.[29]

Chinese and Japanese educational relations reflect a larger concern in both societies for international education. In China, special care is taken also at the higher educational level with the main purpose of training highly specialised personnel and of developing science and technology, with an openness to the past and to foreign countries. The policy guiding educational research in China has been: 'make the past serve the present and foreign things serve China'.[30] A direct influence of Japan is seen in Chinese higher education: To ensure academic standards, the curricula of the principal specialisations taught in universities and colleges are now drawn up by the Ministry of Education on the Japanese and American models.[31]

A Japanese comparative educator has questioned the traditional concept of international education:

As experience has increased, it has become clearer that internationalisation is not just additional or peripheral to the national system; it requires fundamental changes in the existing system . . . Serious reflexion indicates that further quantitative growth without fundamental improvement must be directed in at least two directions — the diversification of the school system and its internationalisation, both of which should bring about a fundamental reorientation of contemporary Japanese education.[32]

The exchange of students and university teachers between the two countries is still limited; however, in the future it might still be worthwhile to study how this exchange has contributed to a more meaningful international co-operation.

As far as Japan is concerned: 'If Japan wants to make a contribution to development in the Asian and Pacific region, it is definitely necessary to encourage cultural exchanges and to increase communication with other nations'.[33] In general, Japan itself is a large net importer in cultural exchanges, and a large exporter of material goods.

Both countries have had periods in their histories where relations with the external world were characterised by foreign domination due, in part, to the technological superiority of those foreign countries.

This common experience is one reason for not speaking of the relationship between China and Japan as that of a North-South relationship. Moreover, because of China's large population and natural resources, Chinese political and economic policies have an influence on agricultural, financial and, to a certain extent, also industrial international markets; for this reason China holds a great deal of political and economic bargaining power. Also we should not forget that: 'One-third of the population of the developing world lives in the PRC, and the lessons of success and error in its efforts will be of wide international concern.'[34]

Notes

1. World Bank, 1982
2. M. Wionczek, 'Power Plays in Asia', *Bulletin of the Atomic Scientists*, no. 3, vol. 39, March 1983
3. S. Kato, *The Japan-China Phenomenon, Conflict or Compatibility?*, Tokyo, Kodansha International Ltd, 1975
4. C. Verceil, 'L'indétermination du Japon — Le scénario de l'alliance avec la Chine', *Problèmes politiques et sociaux*, no. 438, Paris, La Documentation française, April 1982
5. A.Yeats, 'China's Recent Export Performance: Some Basic Features and Policy Implications', *Development and Change*, January 1984
6. M. Lucbert, 'Pékin cherche à attirer les investisseurs japonais', *Le Monde*, 27 March 1984
7. Michio Uga, 'China's New Modernisation Drive', *Journal of Japanese Trade and Industry*, January-February 1983
8. Ibid.
9. Kenji Umeura, 'Settlement Procedures in Japan-China Trade', *China Newsletter*, no. 50, May-June 1984, JETRO (Japan External Trade Organisation), 24
10. Ling Xing-Quang, *Japan Quarterly*, January-March 1982, Tokyo, Asahi Shimbun
11. P.T.K. Lin, 'The People's Republic of China and the NIEO; the Strategy of Domestic Development', *Asia and the New International Economic Order*, London, Pergamon Press, 1981, p. 72
12. T. Mende, *Soleils levants. Le Japon et la Chine*, Paris, Seuil, 1975
13. Ibid.
14. Kiyoji Murala and Isamu Ota, *An Industrial Geography of Japan*, New

York, St Martin's Press, 1980

15. Ling Xing-Quang, 'The Chinese Economy Learns from Japanese Experience', *Japan Quarterly*, January-March 1982, Tokyo

16. S. Pepper, *China's Universities*, Ann Arbor Center for Chinese Studies, The University of Michigan, 1984

17. C. Hoffmann, 'The Urban Unemployment in China', *Asian Thought and Society* no. 25, March 1984

18. Jean-Michel Leclerck, 'Le Japon et son système éducatif', *Notes et études documentaires*, no. 4747-8, Dec. 1983

19. N.J. Colletta, 'Worker-peasant Education in the People's Republic of China', *Chinese Education*, vol. XV, no. 1-2, Spring-Summer 1982

20. M. Bastid, 'Chinese Educational Policies in the 1980s and Economic Development', *The China Quarterly*, no. 98, June 1984

21. Chen Taolei, 'On the Inevitability of Instituting the Dual Education System', *Chinese Education*, Fall-Winter 1980-1, vol. XVI, no. 3-4

22. T. Noguchi, 'High Technology and Industrial Strategies in Japan', *Labour and Society*, vol. 8, no. 4, Oct.-Dec. 1983

23. Y.Z. Luo, *Relations Between Education, Science and Culture and the Mode of Socio-economic Organization and its Development: the Chinese Experience*, Paris, Unesco, 1982, p. 84

24. J.S. Prybyla, 'The Economic System of the People's Republic of China', *Asian Thought and Society*, vol. IX, no. 25, March 1984

25. R. Conroy, 'Technological Innovation in China's Recent Industrialization', *The China Quarterly*, March 1984

26. Dong Fureng, 'Some Problems Concerning China's Strategy in Foreign Economic Relations', *International Social Science Journal*, no. 3, 1983

27. Y. Miyazaki, 'Joint Ventures for China's Development', *Economic Eye*, March 1984

28. Lee Travers , 'Post-1978 Rural Economic Policy and Peasant Income in China', *The China Quarterly*, no. 98, June 1984

28. F.V. Moulder, *Japan, China and the Modern World Economy*, Cambridge, Cambridge University Press, 1977

30. China Handbook Editorial Committee, *Education and Science*, Beijing, Foreign Language Press, 1983

31. M. Bastid, 'Chinese Educational Policies', 193

32. T. Kobayashi, 'Into the 1980s: the Japanese Case', *Comparative Education*, vol. 16, no. 3, Oct. 1980, 244

33. M. Sakamoto, 'Japan and the Nieo., *Asia and the New International Economic Order*, Oxford, Pergamon Press, 1981, p. 25

34. P.T.K. Lin, 'The People's Republic of China and the New International Economic Order: the Strategy of Domestic Development', *Asia and the New Economic Order*, Oxford, Pergamon Press, 1981, p. 25

14 A PERSONAL INTERNATIONAL EXPERIENCE

I would like to share some findings on my experience of international relations in education. First, I have found that economic and technological relations are as relevant as ideological belief for establishing the main ties between countries. Secondly, that people in education at national and international levels are much more creative if they feel more closely bound to the people and to scientific communities rather than just to institutions. Thirdly, that educators need to have a permanent training which is not merely institutional, but has to be developed in real life. Speaking of my personal training experiences, I have to say that I have received more new ideas and findings from people engaged in social and cultural movements than from the educational establishment.

Who is supporting international co-operation? First of all, there are the independent and creative intellectual communities which are capable of understanding international co-operation as a means for the construction of international democracy. They support international co-operation advocating progressive policies and practices in international activities not solely on the basis of their own self-interest, but on that of co-operation leading to development and real justice among countries. Secondly, there are the social and cultural movements which help international innovative practices and call on governments and international organisations to answer the emerging needs of the people in relation to their working and non-working lives, and which refuse to become an instrument for reinforcing international conformity and meaningless compromises on culture and education. Thirdly, there are those in production (industrial and rural workers, managers, union leaders, etc.) who are beginning to question the national and international educational and cultural structures when the latter seem unable to assist them to solve the problems they are facing within the productive system. Fourthly, there are the scientific and artistic creators and researchers who offer new discoveries and produce new cultural values, thereby ridiculing moralistic and rhetorical education and fighting all the various forms of censorship.

Education for international understanding and co-operation is a growing field in many countries: it is possible to find programmes of this nature in universities, in schools, in adult education, but these programmes often need to be radically changed if they are to become meaningful. Today mankind does not need verbal declarations on international understanding or vague intercultural exchanges. It needs concrete, scientific, technical, cultural, economic projects that reinforce the capacity for self-development in the countries on the periphery. For this very reason, education for international co-operation has to be action-oriented, and fully aware of the concrete problems of national and international societies. But we are very far from this approach.

The distribution of the gains from international co-operation will be difficult to achieve without a central redistributive authority,[1] and 'Moreover, an international redistribution might be of little consequence without a redistribution of wealth domestically in each nation'.[2] On one side, international authorities are needed; on the other side, they are under attack and given limited means. Although reports are proliferating throughout the world, one can ask whether there is a will to make this a meaningful exercise. Will these reports be seen as an opportunity for common enterprises, or will they just be used as further excuses for domination? Why should these reports not express the real feelings of people, their needs, their motivations? Yet, even though reports will continue to be presented no decisions will be taken; for international structures are weak, and economically and militarily powerful countries pursue their own interests and continue their conflicts regardless of the recommendations contained within these reports. As a partial reflection of their lack of concern, military expenditure increases much faster than the national income in the most disadvantaged countries.

The dialectics between peoples, governments and international organisations are only just developing. Therefore, there is still a great deal of both idealism and cynicism. On the one hand, people generally do not think it is possible to influence international affairs. On the other, officials of international organisations are often very protective of their international responsibilities and are often separated from reality. People and governments address themselves to international organisations and await magic answers to relevant problems concerning the economy, technology and the environment. International popular participation and self-reliance are increasing, but not many people are aware of this.

Young people in many countries are ready to engage in national and international projects and to react against conservative trends that are inhibiting a more equal development among the different countries of the world. Formal education systems prepare a significant number of qualified young people, but the enthusiasm of the young and qualified is often paralysed because of the lack of work, meaningful projects and creative involvement in their society.

We are presently witnessing a regression regarding policy development, the search for strategical alternatives in the use of natural resources and the creation and reinforcement of activities in the field of international co-operation. In the 1970s there was an interest in new trends. Today it seems that the main concern is to convince wealthy people in the wealthy countries to consume more and more.

Are these trends inevitable? Is it possible to start thinking again of positive alternative approaches to (a) the diffusion of technology, (b) the creation of new services, (c) types of consumption, etc.? Can adult education contribute to the building of an international democracy that results in more equal relations between countries, between social groups and people, and between different civilisations? The achievement of international democracy will be largely the result of new international economic relations, but perhaps education also has its contribution to make, both directly and indirectly.

A new international educational order is a condition and a consequence of new international economic relations. Mankind has a bleak future if the differences created in material conditions and qualities of life are such that people and countries are hard put to understand each other and to communicate among themselves.

Intercultural exchanges can become a relevant new frontier for adult education. People generally have only very superficial knowledge about countries with whom economic co-operation is often growing quite fast. In a closely interrelated world, history and contemporary culture can become a positive way to enrich ourselves without depriving other people. Non-material consumption may be part of the perspective of progress for industrial societies. Creative adult education can become a relevant instrument for the new aesthetic, scientific and progressive adventures of mankind.

In this perspective, educators will need new and relevant cultural training and living cultural experiences; otherwise education can become self-defeating and even an obstacle to education. In several societies, educators are disseminating old values and resisting the new and emerging ones. Educators have to be in close touch with the outside world in order to develop a full and creative use of human resources, but at the same time they have to resist educational guidelines that are imposed on educational structures by those who try to manipulate educational activities.

But who and where are the creative educators? Emerging educational needs are creating relevant educators; leisure time, new systems of production, the obligatory free time of unemployment, mass media and consumption – these are the new time and space for education, and out of this time and space new adult educators with specific practical skills are arising. But these educators who are not employed within the institution are feared because they are provoking 'crisis', 'ruptures', 'doubts' within the educational system and threatening the existing power structures.

Why is there this gap between education supply and the potential users of education? Boredom, an academic façade, vested interest in national and international education networks, bureaucratic resistance – all of these are very strong barriers against relevant educational policies and meaningful education practices. Creative strategies are needed to allow better co-operation between the innovative people in societies and educational institutions.

National, regional and international projects in education are needed to cope with social and cultural demands. Young people are asking for better integration into the social and economic environment. Developing countries are struggling for a more equal share of natural and technical resources, marginal social groups want to be considered an integral part of their society; and still projects are falling short of providing an answer to these demands.

Is adult education capable of generating new ideas, projects and practices? Can traditional adult education institutions come up with new approaches? What can be done to involve the people, movements, individuals, countries who are the new participants in education? How can professional educators work with them without manipulating them?

There is nothing new in the assertion that adult education is becoming an important market for selling and buying education. Demagogy and moral phrases are still used to cover up this reality. To build one's life on the basis of professional education is not **negative**; on the contrary, what is important is to avoid confusion, manipulation and useless activities just because money and power are involved, and many providers and users of education are unaware of the politics and manipulation of education.

Adult educators are often leading their programmes to failure because they have little knowledge of the sociological and anthropological nature of the new education-seekers who are becoming involved in the education process. A serious effort has to be made to qualify educators through theoretical studies, and through field work related to emerging educational needs and to the new sections of the public. The creativity, generosity and openness of adult educators are perhaps the real prerequisites for efficient educational activities: these gifts motivate others and help encourage curiosity, interest and the will to be involved in activities that are often very demanding for both young people and adults.

The crisis affecting school teachers is also affecting adult educators, and the main reason for this crisis is the discrepancy between the knowledge asked for by the students or even possessed by these students, and the knowledge of the educators. Today the generation gap means that older people often lack relevant knowledge of contemporary developments. In many countries adult educators are the inheritors of some resources that in the past were channelled to schools. Is adult education using or misusing these new available funds? What are the differences between the more formal schooling and the less formal adult education? A careful comparative analysis between school and adult education shows that very often conformity, lack of aesthetic values and poor creativity are not peculiar to the school system.

Theory and practice have a dialectical relationship today which implies the need for creativity in both. Contemporary societies ask for new theoretical foundations of education dealing with the new meaning of knowledge and education, as well as of the nature of scientific, technological and educational exchanges. Practice can nourish new theories and, at the same time, needs a wider theoretical background including new disciplines. Adult education, and not just school education, has not moved in this direction. Scientific and technological innovations in education have been very modest indeed because of the cultural, psychological and personal resistance of the 'established' world of education.

One of the main difficulties for educators is to prepare for an uncertain future. Future functions in social, economic and political life are likely to be different from those of today for the great majority of people, and educational institutions have difficulty in forecasting these changes. The revolution of productive structures is accelerating in a way unprecedented in the history of mankind. Perhaps the most urgent task for adult education is, therefore, the introduction of initial training, and not only the retraining of teachers and adult educators. Trade unions, including the teachers' unions, if they truly represent the interests of the people, must welcome these educational trends and not resist them.

The new relevance of education is often not appreciated by educators: education is not only a preparatory activity for work, but is also becoming one of the most relevant productive activities and a significant part of the daily life of everyone. Many people spend as much time in educational activities as they do at work. Educational services, whether independent or integrated with information services, are the most significant part of the productive sector in the field of services, research and development.

What about education as an instrument for resisting and denying education? It seems a paradox, but it can be and is sometimes a reality. Why are so few new educational ideas emerging from the educational establishment? Why are schools and adult education institutions sometimes an instrument for disseminating propaganda and conservative values among youth?

Repression of creativity occurs in the East and in the West, in the North and in the South: education can play either a positive or a negative role in this respect. Educators can become an instrument for normalisation, or they can detect and encourage emerging creativity and new values.

Educational theories are emerging through struggles, observations and various forms of creativity, but they cannot be prescriptive because they have to be tested. Therefore, the contents, methods and techniques of adult education need new consideration.

The contradiction between educational ideologies in the East and in the West and the power and social structures of these societies are giving rise to new educational experiences in several countries that are more consistent with the democratic educational ideologies that are so often proclaimed. 'Flying universities' in the East, 'peace movements' in the West are but two examples of educational practices that are welcomed by an ever increasing number of people who are dissatisfied with the contents and with the social selection imposed by the formal and non-formal educational structures of industrial societies, both 'free market' and 'planned economy'.

I have a strong impression that real educational innovations are the result of the creativity and personal risks taken by people fighting in their social and productive lives to improve working and social conditions for their colleagues and for themselves. It is only after these innovative experiences that the more institutional and academic educational world is ready to think about and to introduce new educational policies and practices. The development of permanent relationships with these creative and motivated people may be the condition for the development of meaningful education.

A bridge between the personal and the political dimension of education has to be established. Too often, these two dimensions are separate. There is education which addresses psychological problems, personal relations, etc., but by contrast there is a political and ideological education which offers a purely deterministic social and economic interpretation of human beings. These two unidimensional approaches lead in many cases to irrelevant education, because something is missing. 'Marx' and 'Freud' are both relevant for educators, but too often one or other of these references is omitted, and the further reaction to this oversight is again a unidimensional approach.

Adult education, at least of the institutional kind, is not coping with emerging knowledge in science, technology, the arts, economics and political economy. The adult educational world is very often a closed one. Therefore, research in adult education, and not only adult educational practices, have also to be developed outside the educational world — with a contribution from people other than educators in the traditional sense, and using scientific methods and avoiding, if possible, traditional educational conformity.

New discoveries in the human and natural sciences, as well as in technology, do not circulate as often as they should within the adult education world. Adult educators are not seen to be familiar enough with the new thinkers, novelists and scientists. Therefore, the political and sociological analysis of adult educators is often weak on national, as well as on international issues. Ignorance, taboos, and prejudices are more frequent among adult educationalists than, for example, among atomic scientists: look at their respective publications and you will be surprised at the differences. Are the latter too relevant and the former too marginal to the main contemporary issues?

New technologies in the productive process are interpreted quite differently as far as the skilling and deskilling of people is concerned. For some researchers the skilling is not a risk, because workers involved in new technologies are exposed to different types of new knowledge. For others, new technologies mean an increase in the commodity status of labour power, but for the moment adult educators are still far from this debate. They seem to be concerned only with the vocational aspect of new technologies.

The redefinition of work is going on in the productive system, because of new technologies, new patterns of organisation, job sharing, etc. But the world of education has some difficulty in understanding these changes and in anticipating the implications. The relationship between work and education is often reduced to adaptation, or vocational training. A concern for more open and creative education is proclaimed, but with poor implications for the educational process. The creation of jobs through education and culture seems to be more a verbal declaration than a real policy.

The world of adult education seems to adapt itself very fast to outside pressure. The transition from liberal to vocational education seems to go on with very limited critical analysis. New models of development (the pure satisfaction of the consumption needs of industrial society) are accepted even if they are in regression with respect to some models proposed in the 1970s. Do adult educators have a voice concerning new values and models of development in our contemporary societies?

The spread of technology is one of the most relevant aspects of international exchange, but is often imposed on countries without any kind of negotiation. International organisations are absent from, or very weak in this field. Technologies and new scientific discoveries are needed and useful if they can be introduced in a fair and coherent way with respect to cultural identity, and to the economic and social development of societies affected by these discoveries within North-South, North-North and South-South relationships. The diffusion of technology has direct implications for further vocational training, but also indirect implications for initial training.

The developing countries are often dissatisfied with the vague educational propositions that are coming from the industrial countries. There are immediate needs, and people want to find educational answers and very concrete ones both within their country and from abroad. International co-operation has to find an answer to these demands, but at the same time countries and international organisations have to acknowledge that new objectives in education require new and coherent contents, methods and techniques. The history of international co-operation in education records many useless activities because of the diffusion of irrelevant educational plans, contents, methodologies and technologies.

Developing countries are not so much interested in finding in comparative education some features to import into their own systems, but ask for a new perspective of education on an international basis. The progressive educators of developing countries ask for more worldwide involvement of the forward-looking people from the industrialised countries. Educational struggles are common to the North and the South and cannot be separated. Sociological analysis shows that new educational policies and practices in most countries can come from within and from outside. Self-sufficiency is no longer possible; therefore comparative education cannot be a purely intellectual analysis of different educational practices and policies.

Comparative education can be, and in some cases is, an instrument for domination and for reinforcing the traditional and conservative educational establishment. New educational experiences are developing all over the world both inside institutions and outside them, but these new experiences very seldom contribute to the progress of the educational systems, because educational information is not always selected according to progressive criteria. The gap between developed and developing countries, concerning information and documentation, is growing fast, and new dependences are developing because of this gap. Adult education models are imposed from outside on many countries because computers and documentation centres are connecting and distributing data coming from only a limited number of countries. Access to information is widening according to the wealth of a country and to the power of individual and social groups. New inequalities are arising within the educational world because of different positions with respect to the access to information.

Progressive people have difficulty in communicating, because national innovations are often censored and repressed at the national and the international level. The cost of international communication means difficulties for creative and independent people to communicate, and to work together.

The building of an international society also needs international curricula for initial and further training. If we look at the content of education in many countries we find that many foreign countries are still presented in a very marginal and folkloric way. Few efforts are made to give a full understanding of other societies. The failures of many adult education programmes, within the framework of international co-operation, have their origin, among other reasons, in the great ignorance of the adult educators who are sent abroad.

'The growing relevance of international activities needs a new type of qualified individual who possesses a full understanding of international life. In many countries there is an explosion of international communication and co-operation, but very often open-minded and qualified personnel are lacking. International exchanges, international civil services and national civil services, open to international life, are becoming a relevant sector of the new services, and adult education can be a part of these new activities.

The growing field of international co-operation has so far established but few rules; therefore, there is a need for some kind of collective self-management through which the people can take responsibility for international co-operation. It is not easy to introduce collective self-management in national or international structures, but it is the only answer, otherwise the lack of involvement decision and concern of wealthy countries for the more peripheral ones can lead to limited, inefficient and marginal international action.

These notes are an invitation to think more creatively on educational relations between North and South and within countries. Theoretical and empirical research are needed; education is not an ordinary commodity to give or to take away. All countries have educational and cultural traditions, and all countries need to develop further their culture and their education.

Notes

1. C. Lindblom, 'Epilogue' in *The New International Economy*, H. Makler, A. Martinelli, N. Smelser (eds), Beverly Hills; London, Sage-ISA, 1982, p. 331
2. Ibid., p. 332

15 CREATIVE STRUGGLES FOR DEVELOPMENT

Educational institutions impose and/or repeat their plans and many educators adapt themselves to them, but happily the exploration of educational reality is always full of promise. This reality is composed of both control and creativity, both in educational institutions and by non-formal education: educators and the educated struggle in the formal and non-formal setting and/or accept and/or are obliged to accept what is imposed upon them; and these impositions, at the local, national and international level, increase in relation to the growing importance of education, of knowledge and of their place in productive and social life.

The contradiction between the institutional offer and educational demand is the most striking fact about education. The offer often represents the reproduction of the educational institution and 'educational violence'; the demand reflects the numerous requirements of societies in transition. Why do institutions and educators seek (or invent) an audience, and why at the same time are children, young people and adults dissatisfied with an education which (a) confines them in a traditional and/or technological and/or cultural illiteracy: (b) is not sensitive to their demand to acquire the means to express themselves at the workplace, in social life, in the family; (c) conveys messages often manipulative, sometimes outmoded, and often not very creative?

A major impasse in the sphere of education is represented by the fact that the most disadvantaged countries and social strata have the most unmet needs, without benefiting from contemporary civilisations. For example, in the area of education countries which may have only a limited control over their economies, and workers who are marginal in the employment market without, or with only limited possibilities for negotiation, are the least able to guarantee formal education to all of their people or, for those who are workers, for themselves and their children.

The response to these problems is often 'aid' at national and international level by specific programmes, and totally insufficient for the real needs of these countries and these marginal people. The correct step to be taken would be by collective international responsibility with the help of all to make the right to education a real right without any discrimination. But how? An international redistribution of means in relation to needs and necessities (and education is one) is one of the conditions. But at the moment, the international division of labour and the ideological domination of the great powers, make education one of the instruments which perpetuate the dependence of some upon the others. Complicity in the field of education has been serious enough; limiting itself to unmasking repression in an institution or in a single country, without concern for the equally serious repression at the international level, suggests more-or-less open complicity in and responsibility for educational repressions. Educators who call themselves progressive in the countries of the North (in America, northern Europe, the Soviet Union and Japan) ought to be questioning their governments and their allies about the actions they are taking, notably in the countries of the South, in the wide field of education, through bilateral, multinational, international co-operation, direct or indirect.

Conflicting and problematic situations are often evaded in educational debates, but educators are confronted with racism, the lack of interest by the marginalised young, a world of production difficult to know and apprehend, profound contradictions between the often moralising and idealistic content of educational institutions, and the direct and/or institutionalised violence present in our societies. If education participates in and is an expression of social life, why avoid situations of conflict?

To understand other cultures signifies accepting the differences and the conflicting situations in them; new syntheses cannot be achieved unless preceded by this acceptance. Often, the educational institution and educational movements tend on the contrary to impose uniformity and morality upon behaviour, and to impose a culture of institutionalised education which is often conservative, conformist, self-perpetuating and, recently, even reactionary.

In a community, in a country, in international society, do we not find a reserve of human resources available for education which are not utilised? An incredible mess is hidden behind the image of the coherence of education systems: unused personal creativity (poets, comedians, sculptors, painters, etc.), creative people active in society but very difficult to use in the education system (scientists, technologists, etc.). Perhaps an education founded upon collective self-reliance would be a better way of valuing existing human resources and responding to the demand for educational activity. The flexibility of educators and institutions, i.e. their response to educational demand, does not threaten their interests; to remain inflexible, that is to say to adapt the learners to the exigencies of institutions and their educators, will achieve little, and is certainly a form of violence.

The impact of education is not only reflected in the relationship of teacher and taught in the school classroom: the mass media, the publishing houses, the information multinationals, international organisations, both governmental and non-governmental, influence education and help to give it a direction. Struggles to reduce the power of these influences might well be denounced as subversive; and will be much more difficult than those which have already taken place in some schools and universities. The possibilities of influence and manipulation by their powerful groups are numerous, and solitary defence is difficult, and collectively very complex.

The conformism of bureaucracies, the 'pallid' fantasy of civil servants and the violence which strikes (when creativity transforms or seeks to transform educational and cultural space and time in evading control) tarnish educational activities. And all the time it is especially in the institutions where the struggle is likely to be denounced as subversive. Qualitative education within the quantitative one signifies a fierce struggle in order that, through popular participation, education of all and by all will be creative, rigorous in its aesthetic dimension, non-repetitive and entertaining. Why, for centuries, should workers have fought to gain the right to a formal education, and today should 'receive' an education without quality and without colour, without perspective and with obligations, uninspired and lacking any *raison d'être*?

Technological development, bound up with economic change at national and international level and with the development of social relations, on the one hand creates the necessity to open up rapidly to the whole of the population the new technological literacy, but on the other seems not to require the contribution of part of that population to productive activities. The extension of secondary and higher education brings about a change in the structure of social relations, founded in the past upon the different educational levels, but the failure to employ the educated young creates new conflicts within existing social-class structures. Furthermore, the education of adults, apart from initial training, has two kinds of public: (a) those who, in education, find alternative occupations to employment, often not wished for; (b) others who, in education, feel the need to find a way to remain in the employment market (retraining, further professional training, etc.).

Facile criticisms of teachers will not much advance education: often those most criticised are teachers who work in the most difficult conditions and with people without or with little hope, and notably in secondary education, with young people who have had no chance of getting themselves into working life, in the neglected regions hit by unemployment, among marginal social groups, etc.). Teachers are often alone in facing the problems which overtake them; it is above all in this context that collective educational actions have a significance because they include the participation of the many existing productive, cultural and social elements in society.

The administrators of education, and the educators themselves are, however, seldom 'creative' in the face of those responsible for the industries of war and the organisation of the military machine: the immense resources of the countries of East and West, of North and South are frittered away by the destructive 'creativity' of the industry and commerce of war. Why is it not possible to envisage a constructive and creative conversion of those means into productive, cultural and educational activities? How to convert these investments in war to creative use for peace is perhaps the most urgent and the most fascinating of all national and international problems.[1] Nuclear researchers, engineers, physicists, chemists should be in the service of mankind to make life richer in progress, inventions, useful discoveries and daily aesthetic pleasures — this conversion is fully possible. The right to leisure, the right to work, the right to freedom of expression, the right to education, the right to health, etc. do not seem to be, unfortunately, the objectives of most educational actions. And that is a pity. As for the moral declarations of and in respect of these rights, education could have a role to play and, at certain times, plays it, but it is rarely spoken of as such.

But when it is, education becomes the action of all, and by all. The strength of education is not weakened by an increase in the number of its objectives, or in the increase in the number of life situations used for education, but on the contrary, in that perspective people will grasp the true relevance of education. They are tired of pedagogical education which speaks and responds so little to their demands and their needs. There are a multitude of examples of education that hold back development.

Fortunately, creative educational movements and educators do exist: and the formal structures of education should establish relations and debate with those in professions other than education. I propose here to mention a few of these 'educators' I know or have met.

(1) Sally N'Dongo,[2] Senegalese, President of the General Union of Senegalese Workers in France (UGTSF), has for 25 years worked for the recognition of individual and collective human rights; education organised by the union plays a part in the training of migrant workers, in the training of villagers, in the training of the people of the country where the migrant worker resides. For the UGTSF and its President, education signifies the struggle for culture, for housing, for the creation of employment and services in their villages of origin, for their own self-respect and that of others. Education, for the UGTSF, must range from basic literacy towards the most general training of migrant workers; it must include training towards participation in national and international political and cultural debates, from participation in these debates towards work in the social, cultural, educational and medical infrastructures in the villages those workers have left behind, and where their families often continue merely to survive in shocking conditions.

(2) Leonardo Zanier,[3] Italian, responsible for the Coop Sind (co-operative organisation) has known in his lifetime a thousand-and-one activities in productive, political, union and educational life: the guiding thread being poetic expression. His educational activity is a ceaseless search for meaning and for the breakthrough to create true solidarities. The achievement of his educational action in professional training, in union work, in co-operative activity, in the creative community is above all to make everyone, in individual and collective terms, master of his work and his choices, and above all capable of creation and production.

(3) Stefano Varese,[4] Peruvian, anthropologist, refuses to limit himself to observing the people with whom and for whom he works. Research is training, for himself as much as for the Indians of Peru and Mexico whom he has come to know and with whose creativity he has become familiar.

(4) Francis Jeanson,[5] French, philosopher, opponent of the Algerian war, writer, former Director of the Maison de la Culture de Châlon sur Saône, interdisciplinary researcher in psychiatric hospitals, embodies an educational approach which is always concerned with responding to the most acute problems in contemporary society.

(5) Andrei Wajda,[6] Polish, has made the cinema a precious instrument of communication and of response to the disquiet of contemporary societies. His films have the great merit of not being didactic, yet of being truly educational.

(6) Rudi Supek,[7] Yugoslav, sociologist, is an example of a teacher who yields neither to pedagogical rhetoric nor to that of ideology. A

Marxist advocate of self-reliance, with a passionate clarity, seeks always
to present reality as it is in his own country and elsewhere, without
compromise and with a permanent hope for humanity; he has the
lucidity and the optimism of someone who has seen death and the
struggle for life in the concentration camp of Buchenwald.

(7) Michael Smith, Jamaican, poet, killed in 1983 after a life of
intense poetical generosity. He was killed perhaps because he was a
great educator. His poetry, integrated into musical expression, has been
and is the permanent source of life, of creativity, of question and
response.

(8) Helma Sanders Brahms,[8] German, film-maker, has made the
building of peace her *raison d'être*. War and the humiliation of 'vic-
tories' and defeats strike at women no less than men, and Helma
Sanders Brahms cries out her will to live, in order that war should disappear and life triumph.

None of these different personalities are educators in the strict
sense of the word, but their activities involve fully the young people
and adults who participate in their work, delighting in their work and
identifying with their quest. Young people and adults testify to a lively
concern, for they ask questions, stimulated into searching for and sug-
gesting solutions. On the other side are the hostility and the envy,
perhaps, of mediocre bureaucrats, hypocrites and above all of the
power groups opposed to these creators who involve themselves with
their publics in a natural, dialectic and spontaneous manner.

Why are these personalities not invited to contribute to pedagogical
reviews, to educational meetings, to 'pedagogical innovation'? Perhaps
it is because they are the true innovators and because they are 'disturbing'. Their particular language, their questioning and their commitment free of rhetoric, demolish the moralising declarations of the pedagogical establishment. Fortunately, history rapidly forgets the censors,
the manipulators, the more or less subtle conformists. But why not
anticipate history now?

These personalities are not solely the result of individual free choice:
they represent currents of thought, of action, of commitment, of
investigation present in our societies which struggle *for* a full utilisation
of human resources, *against* direct or institutional violence, *for* creativity, invention, construction, against boredom, platitudes, closed
societies, the self-perpetuation of powerful groups, in West and East,
North and South.

These creative forces do exist in society, and through them

education can become more creative. Their struggles are the most significant aspect of contemporary education. Academics, both 'formal and non-formal', increase in number, but their training and what they are able to produce does not seem to be sufficient.

I have worked in the field of education for a long time, and I am seeking a new language. Pedagogical communication is often abused, manipulated and retrieved, diverted: there are those who are 'masters' of these operations, in formal and non-formal education, in institutions and outside them. These are not the times for putting things off, for closing our eyes, for going back. Institutional violence alternates with direct violence: racism is becoming more and more manifest and education could have a role to play in destroying it in that it uncovers the fear and, sometimes, the hatred of the different and the unknown. Employment is a problem in the societies of North and South and one thousand million jobs have to be created between now and the end of the century. Education is essential for the creation of employment. Bombs and missiles are multiplying and famines are becoming endemic . . .

Where are the Auditors?

Where are the auditors? Where are the new accountants?
It is life that we credit. Warfare and death are engendered by fear, by
    fear of others.
Where the oneness of opposites fails, let us choose love and creation.
    Violence we reject; we yield to the power of poetry.
The pavement markets bring people together afresh.
    Let work and leisure alike get free of the curse of Adam.
    Why then should work be compulsory?
    Why then should leisure be sinful?
    Why should it be tedious?
Devise a tomorrow freed from the torturer!
    Extinguish the urge to kill!
    Let each month strip away a quantity of dismantled missiles.
    Let the number of prisoners freed be counted.
    Let places of torture be turned into gardens, wells, drinking water
    and food freely available!
Our aims shall prevail; our times of joy no longer an escape into alcoholic stupor; let them be real celebrations, occasions of lasting pleasure!

Friends, let us strive to see all the gaolers, the torturers and the firing
squads without occupation, while the legions of unemployed
people find work for their daily bread.
A hundred thousand more poets!
A hundred thousand fewer generals!
And these millions of litres of milk,
these tons of sugar and corn —
let us exchange them, barter them,
trade them in! Let us compensate for them!
And for these millions of bombs — small, medium, large
(black, red, yellow, green, blue, white, orange).
Where are the new accountants, where are the auditors?
We grieve for their absence, we have great need of them.

Notes

1. M. Barrat Brown, *Arms Industry Conversion. An Adult and Research Project*.
London, Bertrand Russell Peace Foundation, 1983
2. Author, among others, of *Voyage forcé, Itinéraire d'un militant*, Paris,
Maspero, 1975 and *Exil, connais pas*, Paris, Cerf, 1976
3. Author, among others, of *Sboradura e sanc*, Firenze, Nuova Guaraldi, 1981
4. Editor, among others, of 'Etnias y lenguas en Oaxaca', *Cuadernos de Trabajo*,
Oaxaca, M. 1 (Mexico, Dirección, General de Culturas Populares)
5. Author, among others, of *Éloge de la psychiatrie*, Paris, Seuil, 1979
6. Producer, among others, of *l'Homme de marbre*
7. Author of *Imagination* (in Serbo-Croat), Zagreb, Liber, 1980
8. Producer, among others, of *Allemagne, mère blafarde*

16 LIFELONG EDUCATION: OPPORTUNITIES AND OBSTACLES

Trends

During the last ten years the concept of lifelong education has, not without difficulty, begun to be adopted as a principle of educational policy and planning by politicians and educationists: it has been seen not simply as one element of the education system but as a means of transforming it in both its formal and non-formal aspects. This development has signified a new interest in lifelong education for many countries, and not only for those which have associated it with adult vocational education during a period of strong economic growth. On the one hand, however, lifelong education is still conceived in merely tautological or prescriptive terms, without any actual progress or challenge; on the other hand, there is the 'subversive' practice of lifelong education which raises issues about the content, methods and, above all, aims of the educational process; in the curse of this dialectic, lifelong education has become a significant issue in the educational debate.

On the one hand, there is education for development creativity, invention, co-operation, democracy, participation, self-development, the search for significant values, freedom of expression for individuals and groups, the right of everyone to aesthetic experience, the satisfaction of needs both essential and 'non-essential'. On the other, education is an instrument of oppression, control, segregation, intolerance, to a greater or lesser extent covert racism, boredom, bureaucratisation, social reproduction, the triumph of platitudes, moralism, the reification of significant values. It is within this dialectic that, during the 1970s, the struggle developed concerning the research, theory, policy and practice of lifelong education.

The interest during the 1960s and 1970s in lifelong education has been the result of a dialectic (a) in a context of educational policy, notably as between the school system and adult education, and (b) in one of social and economic policy for development, production and the inflexibility of educational structures: from limited practices of adult education in relation to lifelong education, and from a narrow vocational training to a reshaping of the entire educational system in relation to

178

social, economic and technological transformation within different countries. The progress made by the idea of lifelong education in different countries has not been linear, nor has it always necessarily signified a process of democratisation. In the 1960s it appeared to be closely connected with social and technological changes occurring in the industrialised countries; it is only recently that lifelong education has been seen as a major policy option for the entire education systems of other countries too. But is this lifelong education for the development or for the 'de-development' of certain social groups or certain Third World countries?

New and interesting features have arisen concerning those who participate and those who do not participate in education: during the 1970s the non-participants, those on the margin, or those with specific educational problems claimed or were granted the right to formal education (migrant workers, young people awaiting jobs, women seeking employment, the elderly, the handicapped, refugees, the unemployed, etc.); but the entry of these groups into the education system, and particularly into the system of production, has been less evident and often very difficult. In effect, the fundamental step involved in lifelong education, which is that of the relation and/or confrontation between social forces and movements and educational structures, has not often been taken by groups such as these. Consequently, the quantitative and qualitative outcome in terms of democratisation has not been very satisfactory in most countries. Those who have already had access to formal education have been able to continue with it to a higher level; whereas those who have not had such access – or who have had only limited access – to education provision have not been able to benefit from the new educational opportunities. It follows, therefore, that the priority for educational reform is to challenge the system as a whole and not merely to create a parallel provision. Otherwise, in comparing national achievements worldwide, it can be shown that in many education systems short-term innovations, and even sometimes regressive ones, have been identified with the concept of lifelong education; and the social reproduction of these false innovations has been reinforced as an obstacle to democratisation.

The crisis in the content of traditional education, and in the access of new groups to it, has brought about changes in the recruitment, functions and training of educators. The involvement of 'non-teaching' or 'non-professional' educators has increased and, more recently, the joint initial and continuing training of qualified and unqualified educators has been developed. The introduction of productive work into initial training has opened up the structure of schooling to those engaged in production and research and who possess the kind of knowledge and skills not often present in that structure.

In the context of structures there has been a movement away from the construction of 'lifelong education centres' towards action aimed at the transformation of the whole system of formal education and new relations between this system and that of non-formal education. The relations between school and community, and especially with the world of work, have been strengthened, but the relations between the structures of production and of education have continued to be difficult. A new organisation of educational space and time is apparently needed: relations between education and territory, decentralisation, participation; educational leave, the transition from education to work; courses at the workplace; recurrence; overcoming the rigid barriers between education, work, leisure, retirement, etc.

With regard to contents, those most consistent with scientific and technological development and relevant to contemporary problems (disarmament, the peace movement, cultural reations, etc.) begin to be demanded. Relations between the content of schooling and that of non-formal education are apparent in their contradictions. There is an inconsistency (and often a total lack of communication) between the school system and the realities of the living culture in which it exists (scientific, technological, the creativity of daily life, popular culture, etc.). An effort has been made in some countries to strengthen the cultural content of education and to grasp the whole educational dimension of non-working life. The links between education, culture, work and leisure have often been difficult, because of their 'provocative' nature and the bureaucratic resistance of education systems. Exploration of the urban culture, in the workplace, in various leisure-time activities, has nevertheless made it possible to envisage a living content of education which the education system might well aim at.

Among the emergent educational methodologies can be observed: individual and collective self-development, participation, autonomy and self-realisation, creativity, participant enquiry, action-research. The use of such methods has, however, caused some alarm, since it tends to bring into question the hierarchical principles upon which education systems are based, and resistance to such questioning is widespread.

Educational resistances, checks and conflicts have brought into prominence the problem of education for the political elite both at national and international level. The crisis in education has been perceived in relation (a) to the crisis in the ideology of 'linear development', an ideology which characterised the period of growth in the industrialised countries between 1960-70, and (b) at the same time to the new theories of development which were founded upon the new international economic order. The consequences of international economic relations and the international division of labour for the creation and evolution of social classes in industrialised and Third World countries have become more and more evident.

Emergent educational needs, essential and non-essential, individual and collective, have been at the same time both the result and the motive force of new economic, social and cultural dynamics. Lifelong education and its ideologies are apparently closely tied to social and economic reports and to political, religious and social ideologies, as well as to the educational and cultural history of different countries. Lifelong education is precisely at the same time a means both of the liberation and democratisation of education and of domination and reproduction. Obviously, the expansion of education is quantitatively insufficient and qualitatively even more so. The transition from education for all to education for all and by all has proved particularly difficult and has often brought about forms of creativity and/or a greater or lesser degree of repression.

Obstacles and Opportunities

The concept of lifelong education is increasingly accepted in all its dimensions (the education of children, young people and adults, formal and non-formal education, institutional or self-developmental) but educational policies and practices are still very limited, often because of obstacles in the system of production (requiring immediate returns, hierarchical and rigid administrative structures) and/or the educational system (ideological control, social conformism, persisting selective functions, etc.). In most countries an important part of the adult population is excluded from all forms of institutional education; in some countries this exclusion also applies to children and young people in the early stages of their education. Future scenarios for education (blockages, obstacles, opportunities) are linked to the future of relationships in the international division of labour, North-South and East-West relations, co-operation and the strengthening of the food supply to the developing countries, stabilisation of world prices for raw materials, relations between agriculture and light industry in order to meet the needs of the non-industrialised world, etc., the modalities of 'technology-transfer' (which has often until now been achieved by means of war and occupation of countries).

The rapid transformation of the labour market and the processes of production have brought about changes in the agricultural, industrial and service sectors in the North and the South, and in the East and the West. The unsatisfied demands by young people to enter the formal labour market, or for whom there is not enough land to provide agricultural work in the Third World countries; the development of an unofficial labour market in the cities and especially their environs; growing unemployment in the industrialised countries, owing to technological change and not necessarily to economic crisis; the access of women to industrial and service occupations (and the significant increase in female unemployment); the importance of the work of migrant workers; the changing significance of work in the industrialised countries (the refusal of alienation and the choosing of work for survival rather than for its own sake) are all examples of the new situations which have consequences for the education of children, young people and adults. Generally speaking, education systems have responded tardily to these changes and have not come to terms with the nature of the new problems. For example, changes taking place in the various labour markets have implications for the whole of society, but they have only been partially reflected in education systems; the work and education relation continues to be dominated by vocational education, which is only one aspect of the relation. Work experience in schools, as it is organised in many countries, is often very tentative, or often only an anticipation of vocational training.

Of the new connection developing between education, culture and communications, it is communications that seem to be the most important factor in social and international relations. Innovatory methods of relating culture, communications and education have often been confronted with archaic and rigid educational structures incapable of coming to terms with the dynamic which characterises the various ways of communicating cultural action.

Certain groups in society have found themselves faced with new kinds of limitations upon their development and have begun to demand provision: the young unemployed, people preparing for retirement, black economy and other vulnerable workers, refugees, etc. Provision seems often to be a response to the dangers involved in losing the idea of work as a universal human right. But how could education function both to maintain the *status quo* and to provide such groups with the opportunities for education which would make possible their full integration into society? In the meantime, automation, informatisation and bureaucratisation are creating the apparatus of a modern sophisticated education: two kinds of people, two kinds of training and two educational cultures which seldom come into contact with each other. How should we respond to this new dualism in the education system? How is it possible to create education systems which are open to all without discrimination and which provide different opportunities but all of the same quality?

Strong pressures upon education to meet the ambiguous demands of democratisation and individual advancement have brought about in several countries sweeping reforms in the name of lifelong education, but also contradictory educational practices (private schools, education abroad, professional training for individual advancement, etc.) which tend to perpetuate social structures and individual mobility.

Resistance to a flexible lifelong education system is manifested in different ways and by those (institutions and individuals) who regard education as a means of social reproduction, or initiation, and not of democratisation; and those who are opposed, for example, to (a) lifelong education at the work-place which takes the form of self-management (and thus calls into question the power structure); (b) lifelong education by means of mass communication in a two-way direction between consumers and producers; (c) lifelong education of people for active participation in international affairs on a basis of equality between countries; (d) lifelong education inside and outside the apparatuses of the state, the church, the parties, to involve everyone actively in these institutions and in civil society.

Apart from resistance in the systems of production and education, there are other resistances on the part of: teachers (increasing workload and loss of opportunities for promotion); particular social groups (fearing the democratisation of schooling and the introduction of educational equality); and political elements (the risk of losing hegemonic control over their own supporters and eventually over society). The blocking of numerous educational reforms has its origin not only in the resistance of those opposed to social and economic change, and consequently to educational change, but also sometimes in the incapacity of certain social tendencies which have implications for educational reform. Social movements, the unmet collective needs (educational and cultural) of workers, the reaction of ordinary families to educational selection, are among the principal reasons for educational reform, but in the course of working for these reforms the representatives of these forces (unions, cultural movements, political parties, intellectuals, etc.) are often absent, or else they delegate the implementation of reforms to administrators or to the teachers' unions themselves.

Resistance is often provoked by the fear of introducing individual and collective creativity into educational activities. Repression in education has manifested itself at different levels in different countries (the denial of social science teaching in some countries is only one of such manifestations).

One source of educational creativity is the individual and collective contribution of artists, scientists and, in a different way, the masses, but it is directly in opposition to this kind of creativity that criticism of education is aroused sometimes in a repressive way and sometimes in a more subtle and manipulative one. Children and young people are interested in poetry, in theatre, in discovery for its own sake, and often the relation between education and creativity is made difficult (especially since creativity does not obey official rules). Happily however, as far as the arts are concerned, in one way or another, artists find possible ways of communicating, especially with the young. The relation between the world of education and that of scientific research is more difficult. In effect, under different conditions, information about discoveries concerning the more disquieting results of scientific and military research is limited and sometimes difficult to obtain.

It is interesting to pursue the concept of lifelong education in the formation of educational policies: the educational significance of the way in which cultural, social and political struggles are translated into political policy by way of economic, political and union pressures to end up as administrative decisions of the state. Unfortunately, those responsible for educational innovation are only rarely involved at the judicial and administrative decision-making stage and in the daily working of the educational system.

Issues for Research

The ephemeral character of definition of lifelong education, which needs to be more sharply defined, has been confirmed during the last decade: lifelong education – continuing professional education; life education – literacy campaigns; lifelong education – adult education; lifelong education – university extension; lifelong education – self-realisation. There has been an increasing awareness that all these different educational activities are aspects of lifelong education, but that each taken separately does not constitute the whole of lifelong education.

The historical dimension of the concept and practices of lifelong education has become more specific, so that there is a risk of using it in an unhistorical way. The idea of a struggle over the subject matter of education becomes apparent whenever lifelong education projects are formulated, imposed without popular participation, or as a result of action by people claiming their rights to education and collective self-determination.

There is the question of research methods in lifelong education. The choice of one definition or another of lifelong education has consequences for the methods to be used in research, in the evaluation of lifelong education policies and activities and for the evolution of the concept itself. Depending upon whether lifelong education is conceived as an absolute value, a concept, a political idea, an activity, a process, the field of analysis is enlarged.

Lifelong education as an absolute value: research into cultural and educational values makes necessary the indispensable contribution of anthropologists and philosophers.

Lifelong education as a concept: a study of ideologies and their application is a preliminary of this perspective in order to understand an ideology or ideologies of lifelong education in relation to social groups, countries, and to sectors of production in the whole of a given population.

Lifelong education as a political idea and as a policy: for the development of this dimension of lifelong education, political decision-makers, planners, educational administrators all have contributions to make, in that research is necessary which could account for the various intervening factors in educational policy decisions.

Lifelong education as an activity and a process: in so far as this concerns the educational act itself, it is the whole of the population that would have to be questioned to discover their day-to-day educational needs, motivations and opportunities.

Operationalising the concept of lifelong education at the level of educational policies and structures has made it possible to locate it better in a historical, social and economic framework. Reflection, research and educational experimentation have also made it possible to see the implications of the concept for the location, timing, contents and methods of education. Major transformations of the system of production (crisis and development in technology, alienation and unemployment) have tended especially in recent years in the industrialised countries to replace to some extent the primary objective of educational activity, as the sole preparation for production, with a broader education to respond to the complex problems of changing societies. On the other hand, in the industrialising societies, characterised by models of schooling totally separated from productive structures, the new orientations in the subject matter of education have reflected very closely those aspects of education relevant to productive activities.

Research into the subject matter of lifelong education, dominated in the past by theory and philosophy, is beginning to be centred today much more upon the policies and strategies of education, upon the relations between the system of production and the system of educa-education, upon creativity, upon the practical modalities concerning the organisation of the timing and location of education, upon the relations between formal and non-formal education, upon the content of education, and upon the relations between education, animation and cultural action. The vast potential for education in the means of mass communication is also reflected in the literature of this area. But the evaluation of the educational implications of the media of mass communication (radio, cinema, theatre, television, etc.) seems to be restricted to those programmes formally designated as educational. In effect, the explosion of the media of mass communication and information systems has educational implications well beyond the formal educational programmes (radio and television). The media of mass communication not only introduce new contents but above all create new methods of approaching and focusing information. The restriction, and rigidity of certain sources of information for the media of communication (notably the army, industry, etc.) and the high level of competence required to understand it seem to be obstacles for the world of education in becoming more familiar with communication.

Delay in the discussion of education systems and their specific components has stimulated the prospects for research. Timidity has always characterised this research because certain decisive variables concerning the future development of educational systems have not been sufficiently taken into consideration: disruption of productive systems, social relations within the country, increasing military power, tendencies in the international division of labour, the evolution of repressions and freedoms in each society, and the reciprocal relations of these different elements. Above all, there are those demographic projections and forecasts of technological development which have figured as the most important variables in prospective studies, and other dynamics have been neglected.

The cultural contribution of different societies and social groups to the subject matter of education is often underestimated and little studied. The growing awareness of the crisis in the school system in many countries is only one aspect of the 'new educational initiatives', perhaps the negative aspect in the dialectic of the construction of a new educational system. The positive aspects are: individual and collective experience of self-determination, the 'pedagogical' revolt, the creative education of daily necessity and emergence, etc. The qualitative contradiction between these non-institutional tendencies on the one hand, and pedagogical discourse and the various kinds of research and institutionalised education on the other, is often very great, and the originators of these tendencies find themselves at odds with the majority of educational institutions and with those engaged in educational research.

Manipulations, Creativities and Prospects

It might be asked why researchers and educationists have waited so many years to understand the potential of 'manipulation' and of 'creation' contained in the policies and practices of lifelong education? Why have they so lately discovered the projects of political and cultural innovators, for education has not anticipated and accompanied such projects? Why has education been and remains 'for later'? 'But this is Utopian' say those who, similarly, argue that social, political and cultural projects are not understood by the people. The difficulty of this education which anticipates and accompanies transformation is alarming, for it cannot be solely general, nor solely vocational, nor solely political, and the relation between its different elements can have surprising results for everyone.

Training in the most complex societies, in North and South, in East and West, and contributing to the democratic transformation of these societies in respect of human rights, both individual and collective (from war to peace, from unemployment to work for all, from marginalisation to the full participation of all in the life of society, from repression to the individual and collective fulfilment of all individuals and all peoples): lifelong education could be an instrument (but not the only one, and itself ambiguous) of this development in contemporary societies. But the manipulative possibilities of lifelong education are also numerous:

(1) by using the richness of the concept, reflecting the creativity of its social origins (popular culture, workers' education, education for autonomous learning, etc.) to mystify the educational process and to fail to respond to the new qualitative and quantitative needs of the people;
(2) by submerging non-formal education into formal education and by reducing all forms of support for non-formal education on the grounds that it is 'subversive', 'independent', 'creative';
(3) by strengthening lifelong education within the already privileged sectors of the education system (universities, vocational training for better positions in the labour market) and further weakening those which are already weak (primary and early secondary education, education of poorly educated adults, popular education, etc.);
(4) by confusing lifelong education with the non-formal education of the 'underprivileged' in such a way that it is the least expensive means of setting up a democratic system of education for all of the people;
(5) by reducing lifelong education to a system of mass communication and making it necessary for Third World countries to buy software and hardware;
(6) by imposing the cultural values and ways of life of one social class or group upon another;
(7) by feeding the rhetoric of pedagogy, propping up the institutional apparatus, in order to cover up the crisis in education systems (cultural and social movements, students, educators, parents, etc.);
(8) by creating networks of which the function is not the exchange of information but the imposition of cultural and pedagogical hegemony by one country upon another.

In countries and in international co-operation it is necessary not only to promote the concept of lifelong education (or non-formal education, or adult education), but also to discover the more or less conscious plans of whoever are responsible for educational policy and institutions and who, in availing themselves of new educational ideas, develop activities which run counter to them (besides, the rapid expansion of certain areas of non-formal education is also in certain cases a way of introducing people without any specific competence, and sometimes manipulable, and sometimes more submissive than the teachers and professors).

It is necessary to develop (in seeking to avoid the various kinds of manipulation) educational policies and research which are of significance for the pursuit of peace, ecological balance, the transformation of systems of production, the cultural values of work and leisure, respect for individual and collective human rights, the discoveries of science and technology, the participation by people in the life of their societies, greater justice in economic and cultural international relations, and above all creativeness in educational and cultural matters. Lifelong education will be in this perspective a source of co-operative and interdisciplinary work amongst researchers, practitioners and users of educational structures. The difficulties of intellectual co-operation in countries and at the international level are really in confronting the difficulties of giving a new significance to research in the subject matter of lifelong education, research which has already shown signs of involution or a failure to evolve which reflects censorship, self-censorship and manipulations of national and international administrative structures, and the timidity and conservatism of academic structures, researchers and educators.

END NOTE

I would like in this end-piece to share some reflections that are based on my experiences in the international world of education, in my own country and in other countries, and in international organisations and associations. I have had a wide variety of experiences during my professional educational life in secondary and higher education, in national and international organisations, in consultancies, and freelance work. For me, the central problem has always been to see the relations between what institutional education offers and the actual educational needs of people: within this context, false conclusions have been drawn which have resulted in action that works against the needs of people. These conclusions are dangerous and deceiving: to be meaningful in education, sometimes, requires that one be resistant to pressures for conformism and other forms of manipulation. But how is one to act in a meaningful way? First of all, one has to be ready to be in a minority and, sometimes, even to act alone. When conformism prevails, one has to try to be as creative as possible. In the following paragraphs some examples of current struggles in education are noted; in universities, in international educational networks (societies, associations and formal networks) and in international organisations.

In many universities, the fight is on to establish the right to research and teach topics that are relevant to contemporary societies; the right to invite qualified people from both within and outside the academic world to contribute to formally organised seminars; a shift from a purely summative evaluation of learning to a more formative one; the development of teaching founded on research rather than only upon academic readings; increased communication between the worlds of the arts and sciences; institutions facing up to local, national and international reality, the development of closer links with the world of production. Are all these struggles individual or collective adventures? They can be either, depending upon the situation.

Today, networks are seen as magical means for achieving desired change in all spheres of life. Institutional and professional networks are also developing within education in an attempt to overcome the absence of information flows necessary for the generalisation of creative experiences. But networks are not always the best answer! They can come to reflect the vested interests of the institutions that are

creating them. Analysis of the experiences of several presently existing networks is revealing: their experiences are very similar and they
seem rather to promote and/or impose ideas instead of encouraging
creativity and experimentaion. In effect, the professional networks are
often instruments for imposing the views of specific educational groups
or countries: sometimes, the net result is the downright exclusion of
particular peoples and groups. To avoid these negative consequences
it is best to encourage continuous and open exchanges of experiences,
peoples, professional and non-professional educators both within and
between countries, both in co-operation with networks and as alternatives to them.

Stable and formally organised networks of different groups, organisations and people are necessary only when there are concrete and
meaningful problems that require collaborative work: they should not
be used merely as a means of gaining international recognition. Specialised research, educational activities and struggles against manipulation
can all be reinforced through the joint efforts of people who share
some common values and who want to keep their creativity and innovative activities alive. From this perspective, it is meaningful to be a
member of flexible national and international groups and associations
that make no pretention to be representative of the world of education.

How can one be creative within international organisations? Certain
activities are of fundamental importance if continued creativity is to be
the goal: for example, the study of the cultural economic and political
life of different countries rather than simply one's own discipline;
involvement in the intellectual life of the various countries; the elabora-
tion and promotion of educational policies that reflect the aspirations
of people within national and international communities for peace,
individual and collective human rights, aesthetic values, etc. It is necessary to be involved in these activities regardless of the pressure of individuals and groups.

But what are the risks of those who do not have security of tenure
in their posts? What kinds of reactions can be foreseen? They can be
either of a mild or a vigorous nature; involvement has to be of an individual nature, but one also needs to find allies — people working together
can more readily stick to chosen international goals and enjoy intellectual freedom. Hence alternative and non-formal networks may be
possible instruments for creative expression. If such networks are to
encourage expression and creativity the people in charge of them must
not accept manipulative and constricting regulations. Alternative networks should seek to attract the most promising and creative people,

people who have very high intellectual potential and who do not identify their interests with the continued existence of networks. Moreover, the networks should be structured so they can be dissolved once their contributions are no longer needed.

Intellectual life at the national and international level is often a creative struggle, a struggle for independent thinking, but also a struggle to prepare oneself to understand and work with the radical worldwide changes in production and communication that will result from the ongoing scientific and technological revolution. Intellectual creativity needs much patient study, a passion for research and work, and also the strength to be detached enough to look beyond immediate concerns.

Those seeking intellectual creativity and transformative action must be prepared to be ignored, and to be attacked in subtle and even hidden ways. At the same time, the powers who dominate at both national and international level are very often in ideological conflict between themselves. These conflicts can be beneficial to those fighting intellectual struggles, for, amidst the conflict, there is room to express oneself and to communicate one's thoughts.

When working in educational institutions at local, national or international level it is important not to forget that many ordinary people support the creative work that is under way. Keeping this in mind helps one to react against rhetorical language and/or meaningless bureaucratic procedures. Remembering the people for whom and with whom one is struggling to build a world that is more just, makes it easier to be motivated and to enjoy one's work.

In my work I have had the opportunity to meet some wonderful and generous people who have inspired me to continue to struggle at the international level. I have also met the manipulative people who have made me wary of international activities. If I am still fighting it is because I have seen some of the positive results of international co-operation. But I have learned to be sharper in my judgement of people and actions because there are great risks when organising practical activities of becoming an indirect accomplice to the manipulators. International co-operation in education is not a game for innocents. Theoretical and empirical analyses of the political, economic and cultural spheres must go hand in hand if one is to come to a correct understanding of the conflicting forces operating within international relations. One cannot and must not become a prisoner of one's discipline (e.g. in my case, lifelong education) or ignore the negative implications of operations which only refer nominally to one's discipline.

Is it worth, then, carrying out such international work? If so, why?

My own response is that work at the international level is important because it contributes to the creation and opening of areas in which people and 'countries' can meet, share ideas and manifest their oppositions and agreements. Although it is possible to be manipulated, it is also possible to denounce international manipulation, the logic of antagonistic blocs or the vested interests of bureaucratic groups. The permanent creation of international structures has a long way to go. Justified and unjustified attacks will continue to accompany their development in the decades to come. To be part of such a project is not easy — it is both rewarding and frustrating. It is a human endeavour that can contribute either to the liberation or to the continued dependence of peoples and countries.

Are educational prescriptions then meaningful today? How is it possible to intervene in the international division of labour? How can action help to change educational activities and policies? The complexity of international economic and political relations does not have to prevent individuals from everyday educational creativity. The multipolarities of our contemporary world and the multidimensional aspects of education are new challenges to our engagements. We have both to face and to create new educational and cultural experiences. Stimulations and obstacles will be many and varied. These will make some pessimistic, but I am optimist:

There are pessimistic people
those that cannot take
the pressures life hands out to them:
eventually they break.

We have to run the gauntlet,
we conquer and we master,
and when the devil chases us
we carry on, but faster.

There are those called optimistic —
I know for I am one;
we keep on fighting battles
as though they've just begun.

We battle through the night time
we battle through the day
we battle on regardless
for survival come what may.

We take life as it's given
and strive from day to day;
all obstacles we challenge
as they stand in our way.

But pessimistic people
think the rest of us are cruel,
for they are blind — they cannot
   see
survival is the rule.

The game of life just can't be
    bought,
the way is ours to choose,
so we must fight life's battlefield
(we'll fight it all our worth)

and when our lives are over
we'll have left our mark on
    earth . . .

Jordan Burgess Coates[1]

Thus, what international education needs mostly is non-conformism, critical approach and independent thinking. Unfortunately, the world of education is often closed and the dialogue is often a purely internal one. However, I do not wish this to be the case with this book. Hence, I will be pleased to enter into dialogue with any reader who wishes to criticise or comment upon the ideas in it, or who wishes to suggest ways of creating new international educational policies and practices.

Note

1. In *Hard Lines, New Poetry and Prose*, London, Faber & Faber Ltd, 1983, p. 51.

SUGGESTED READING

Abdel-Malek, A. Cao Tri Huynh, Rosier B. and Lê Thành Khôi, *Clés pour une stratégie nouvelle de développement*, Paris, Éditions ouvrières/Unesco, 1984

Adam, G., *Perception Consciousness Memory — Reflections of a Biologist*, Budapest, Akadémiai Kiado, 1980

Adams, F. and Horton, M. *Unearthing Seeds of Fire: the Idea of Highlander*, Winston-Salem (North Carolina) John F. Blair, 1975

Allal, T., Bufford, J.P. Marié, M. and Regazzola, T., *Situations migratoires*, Paris, Éditions Galilée, 1977

Amin, S. Arrighi, G., Gunder Frank A. and Wallerstein, I., *Dynamics of Global Crisis*, New York, Monthly Review Press, 1982

Asp, I. *Development Education Among Trade Unions*, Geneva, United Nations Non-government Liaison Service, 1984, mimeo

Barrat Brown, M. *Arms Industry Conversion. An Adult and Research Project*, London, Bertrand Rusell Peace Foundation, 1983

Bonanni, C. *Education for Human Needs*, New Delhi, Indian Adult Education Association, 1982

Braillard, P. and Djalili, M-R., *Tiers-monde et relations internationales*, Paris, Masson, 1984

Bull, A., Holt G. and Lilly, M., *Biotechnologie — Tendances et perspectives internationales*, Paris, OCDE, 1982

Carpentier, D., *Le transfert en formation*, Paris, Publications de la Sorbonne, 1984

Centre d'études prospectives et d'informations internationales, *Economie mondiale: la montée des tensions*, Rapport du Centre d'Etudes Prospectives et d'Informations Internationales, Paris, Economica, 1983

Centre Royaumont pour une science de l'homme, *Théories du langage, théories de l'apprentissage*, Paris, Seuil, 1979

'Crises and Conflicts — the Case of Poland 1980-81', *Sisyphus Sociological Studies*, vol. III, Warsaw, Polish Scientific Publishers, 1982

Debeauvais, M. (ed.), 'Le rôle des comparaisons internationales dans. les réformes de l'éducation', *Revue française de l'éducation*, 1985

Dia, M., *Dialogue des nations*, Alger, Société nationale d'édition et de diffusion, 1980

——— , *Islam, sociétés africaines et culture industrielle*, Dakar, Les nouvelles éditions africaines, 1975

Dube, S.C., *Development Perspectives for the 1980s*, New Delhi, Abhinav/UN, 1983

Emmanuel, A., *Technologie appropriée ou technologie sous-développée?* Paris, Institut de Recherche et d'information sur les Multinationales/PUF, 1981

Ernst, D., *The New International Division of Labour, Technology and Under-development*, Frankfurt, Campus Verlag, 1980

Friedericks G. and Schaff, A., *Microelectronics and Society for Better and for Worse*, London, Pergamon Press, 1982

Fröbel, F. Heinrichs, J. and Kreye, O., *The New International Division of Labour*, Cambridge, Cambridge University Press/Paris, Editions de la Maison des sciences de l'homme, 1980

Gauhar, A., *Talking About Development*, London, Third World Foundation, 1983

Gorz, A., *Adieux au prolétariat. Au-delà du socialisme*, Paris, Éditions Galilée, 1980

Griebine, A., *La nouvelle économie internationale*, Paris, PUF, 1980

Griffin, A., *Curriculum Theory in Adult and Lifelong Education*, London, Croom Helm, 1983

Hankel, W., 'The Financial Crisis Between North and South. Reasons, Lessons, Conclusions', *Economics*, Institute for Scientific Cooperation, Tubingen, 1984, 7-41

Hauser, R., *A New Beginning for the Unemployed*, London, The Institute of Social Research, 1981

ILO, *New Technologies: Their Impact on Employment and the Working Environment*, Geneva, ILO, 1982

ILO, *World Labour Report*, Geneva, 1984

Ires CGIL (ed.), *Obiettivo democrazia industriale*, Rome, ESI, 1980

Jeanson, F. *L'action culturelle dans la cité*, Paris, Seuil, 1973

——, *Eloge de la psychiatrie*, Paris, Seuil, 1979

Jarvis, P., *A Sociology of Adult and Continuing Education*, London, Croom Helm, 1985

Kaplinsky, R., *Automation, the Technology and the Society*, London, Longmans, 1984

Ki Zerbo, J., *Histoire générale de l'Afrique – I: Méthodologie et préhistoire africaine*, Paris, Stock-Unesco, 1980

Killick, T., (director and editor), *The Question for Economic Mobilisation: the IMF and the Third World*, London, Heinemann, 1984

Lavigne, M., (études coordonnées par), *Stratégies des pays socialistes dans l'échange international*, Paris, Economica, 1980

Le Boterf, G., *L'enquête participation en question*, Paris, Edilig, 1981

Mahler, F., *Introducere in juventologie*, Bucarest, Editura Stintifica si Enciclopedica, 1983

Makler, H., Martinelli, A. and Smelser, N., *The New International Economy*, London, Sage, 1982

Majstorovic, S., *Kultura i demokratija* (Culture and Democracy), Belgrade, Prosveta, 1978

Morin, E., *Pour sortir du XXème siècle*, Paris, Nathan, 1981

N'Dongo, S., *Exil, connais pas*, Paris, Cerf, 1976

————, *Voyage forcé, Itinéraire d'un militant*, Paris, Maspero, 1975

OCDE, *OCDE Science and Technology Indicators Resources Devoted to Research and Development*, Paris, OCDE, 1984

ONUDI, *L'industrie dans un monde en mutation*, New York, United Nations, 1983

Pasinetti, L.C., *Structural Change and Economic Growth*, Cambridge, University Press, 1981

Perulli, P. and Trentin, B., (eds), *Il sindacato nella recessione*, Bari, De Donato, 1983

Prebisch, R., *Capitalismo periferico, Crisis y transformacion*, México, Fondo de cultura economica, 1981

Rama, G., (ed.), *Educación y sociedad en América latina y el Caribe*, Unicef, 'Proyecto "desarrollo y educación en América latina y el Caribe"', 1980

Ruddock, R., *Ideologies – Five Exploratory Lectures*, Manchester, The University, 1981

Sanchez Gordillo, J.M. *Marinaleda, Andaluces, Levantaos*, Granada, Alyibe, 1980

Sewart, A., *et al.* (eds), *Distance Education: International Perspectives*, London, Croom Helm, 1983

Sid-Ahmed, A., *Nord-sud: les enjeux*, Paris, Éditions publisud, 1980

Sirvent, M-T. and Brusilovsky, S.L., *Diagnostico socio-cultural de la población Bernal-Don Bosco*, Bernal (Argentina), Asociación cultural Mariano Moreno, 1978

Stanovnik, J., *Towards the New International Economic Order*, Belgrade Jugoslovenska Stvarnost, Medjunarodna Politica, 1979

Stoneman, P., *The Economic Analysis of Technological Change*, Oxford, Oxford University Press, 1983

Suchodolski, B., *Permanent Education and Creativity*, J. Kuczynski, *Creativity as a Practical Philosophy*, Paris, Unesco, ED-82/WS/16, January 1982, mimeo

Supek, R., *L'imagination* (in Serbo-Croat), Zagreb, Liber, 1980

Turchenko, V., *The Scientific and Technological Revolution and the Revolution in Education*, Moscow, Progress Publishers, 1976

Unesco, *Voix multiples, un seul monde*, Paris, Unesco, La documentation française/Nouvelles éditions africaines, 1980

United Nations, *Overcoming Economic Disorder*, New York, Department of International Economic and Social Affairs, 1983

United Nations, *World Economic Survey*, New York, 1984

Van Rensburg, P., *Looking Forward from Serowe*, Gaborone (Botswana), The Foundation of Education with Production, 1984

Varese, S., (ed.), 'Etnias y lenguas en Oaxaca', *Cuadernos de Trabajo*, Oaxaca, no. 1 (Mexico, Dirección general de culturas populares)

Various authors, 'Education and the New International Economic Order', *International Review of Education*, no. 4, 1982

Various authors 'Education permanente et division internationale du travail', *Education et société*, no. 6, April-May 1984

Various authors, 'L'era dei computers', Ulisse, Anno XXXVIII, Vol. XVI, Fasc. XCVI, Febbraio 1984

Various authors, *Tecnologia, cultura del lavoro e professionalita*, Milan, Franco Angeli Editore, 1981

Various authors, 'The World Economy: Theory and Reality', *International Social Science Journal*, no. 97, Unesco, Vol. XXV, no. 3, 1983

Various authors, *Vers quel nouvel ordre mondial?* (Bulletins du colloque), Paris, Université Paris VIII, Département d'économie politique, 1983

Visalberghi A., (ed.), *Educazione alla pace e scienze dell'uomo*, Firenze, La Nuova Italia, 1985

—— , (ed.), *Quale società, un dibattito interdisciplinare sui mutamenti della divisione sociale del lavoro e sulle loro implicazioni educative*, Firenze, La Nuova Italia, 1984

World Bank, *World Development Report*, Oxford, Oxford University Press, 1984

Zanier, L., *Sboradura e sanc.*, Firenze, Nuova Guaraldi, 1981

INDEX

access to education 101, 113, 179
action, co-operation and conflict
    117-89
    see also development, creative;
        encounters; human sciences;
        international; lifelong
actors in lifelong education 15-16
administration of education 127
adult education 93-4, 172, 178
    exclusion from 181
    international co-operation 163-4,
        166-7
    workers 71-9, 154
Africa 7
    colonial education 56
    competition 35
    co-operatives 66
    'de-industrialisation' 31
    Gross Domestic Product 28-30
    labour force 35
    refugees 98
    research in 145-6
    urban population 84
agricultural decline 34-5
aid, foreign 56, 151, 170-1
    see also developing countries,
        relationships with
        industrialised
aim and concept of lifelong
    education 7-16
all, education for 9-10, 128
alternative education 126-8
Amin, J. 69
Argentina 85
arms industry and race 32, 38, 173
    education as alternative to 138-9
Arrighi, G. 69
Asia
    automation in 51
    competition in 30, 35
    Gross Domestic Product 28-30
    imports, educational 56
    intercultural relations 149-59
    labour force 35
    unemployment 62, 65
assessment 124
associations, community

development 94-5
authorities and inequality 119
automation *see* technology
avant-garde 88

basic education 126
Belgium 62
Brazil 45, 85

Canada 35, 62, 87
    see also North America
capital
    investment 39, 55, 156-7
    mobility 46
censorship 147
centralisation 156
change
    in education 122-6, 157
    in employment 90, 139-40, 182
    in family 77, 113, 152
    fear of 123
    see also new
China 29, 35, 56
    intercultural relations with Japan
        149-59
cinema 88
    city *see* urban
class, social 38
    boundaries blurred 85
    and culture 85, 87-8
    different relations 28
    middle 63
    and mobility 49
    unstructured 53
    see also working class
Coates, J.B. 194
coexistence 19-20
collectives *see* co-operation
colonialism 142, 143
    new and neo- 56, 142, 145
COMECON 30, 38
communications, development of 17,
    73, 78, 182
    see also mass media; technology
community 18, 85, 93-6
computers 51, 72, 101
    see also technology

concept and aim of lifelong
     education 7-16
conflict *see* action etc.
confrontation *see* encounters etc.
consciousness, social 144
consumption
     in China 156-7
     cultural 86-7
     education in 75
controls 124-5, 136
     see also domination
co-operation, need for 33
     see also action etc.; international
          co-operation
co-operatives
     education 74-5
     unemployment 64-6
costs
     education and training 39, 56,
          119
     unemployment 52
creation, job *see* employment
creative/creativity 42, 134-5, 178,
     184, 191-2
     development, struggles for 170-7
     educators 171, 173-5
     international co-operation 160,
          163-5
     lifelong education 187-9
     migration and 97-104
     repression of 165
crisis, global *see* unemployment
crisis in education 180-1
cultural/culture 89, 120, 184
     characteristics of work 45
     of daily life 18, 111
     environment 83-96; community
          development 93-6; rural 90-3;
          urban 83-90
     exchanges, China and Japan
          149-59
     folk 18, 77-8, 86-7
     identity 56, 131-2; lacking 19
     independence 21
     institutions 124
     needs, emerging 105-15
     new 18-19
     oral 111, 134
     policy 86-7
     re-appropriation 18, 41
     representatives, migrants seen as
          98
     search for and importance of
          81-115; emerging needs

          105-15; migration and
               creativities 97-104
     sub- 63-4
cultures
     contemporary, meaning of life
          and history 17-21
     different, co-existence of 19-20
curricula, new, need for 110-11,
     135-6, 168
cybernetics 50
     see also computers; technology

daily life, culture of 18, 111
decentralisation 155-7
'de-industrialisation' 31
demand
     educational 170
     side factors and division of labour
          153
demography
     and migration 101
     and mobility 109
     rural 90
     and technology 50
     and unemployment 63
Denmark 98
dependence, educational 37, 130-2,
     137, 142, 144-5, 171
     see also imports
developed countries *see* industrialised
developing countries
     creativity, limited 134
     culture 120-1, 124
     dependence 37, 130-2, 137, 142,
          144-5, 171; *see also* imports
     education in 40-2, 56; inequality
          119-21
     international division of labour
          25-44
     labour-force structure 34-5
     leaders 145
     literacy and enrolment 36-7
     migration from 32, 37-8, 46, 63,
          98-103, 135-6
     needs, unmet 170-1
     output and GDP 28-31, 34-5, 37
     relationships with industrialised
          countries 33-4, 46, 86; human
          sciences and 141-8; *see also*
          China and Japan
     relationships within 33-4
     research in 40; need for 145-6
     technology, new 55-6, 58
     unemployment in 63, 66

urban population 84
working class movements and
    trade unions 39, 73-4
see also international; oil-
    exporting
development
    creative, struggles for 170-7
    educational 109-10
    new needs and goals 72
    programmes 143
discrimination, positive educational
    75
division of labour, international
    25-44, 152-3
domination 7-9, 17
    see also control

East *see* Asia; developing countries;
    industrialised countries
economic
    aspects of higher education
        133-40
    crises 58
    de-colonisation 46
    enclaves 98-9
    evaluation of educational results
        90-1
    international relations 45-6, 162
    and technological dynamics
        23-79; international division
        of labour 25-44; mobility
        45-60; unemployment 61-7;
        workers' education 71-9
economics, law of 146-7
economies *see* market; planned
ecosystem, damaged 50
education, lifelong *see* action etc.;
    concept; cultural; economic;
    international; meaning of life;
    opportunities
educators
    creative 171, 173-5
    criticised 172
    international co-operation 162-4
    new 77-8
    non-professional 173-5, 179
    obstacles to change 123
    progressive 137-8, 171, 173-5
    training 78, 160, 179
emigration *see* migration; mobility
Emmanuel, A. 55-6
employment
    changes 90, 139-40, 182
    creation of 39, 52-3, 55, 67-9,

119
    informal 38, 65, 68, 107
    and leisure dichotomy 72
    policy 65-6, 68, 76
    productive sector shares of 35
    redefinition 166-7
    seasonal 66-7
    technology, new 51-3
    temporary 66
    of women 63
    see also labour; unemployment;
        work
encounters and confrontation in
    education 119-21
    inequality 119-21
    models, changing 122-6
    possible and 'impossible' alter-
        natives 126-8
enrolment rates 36
environment of culture *see* culture
equality 142
    see also inequality
ethnic minorities 143-4
    see also migration; mobility
Europe
    competition in 38, 45
    co-operatives 64-6
    cultural initiatives 89
    education 38, 174-5
    educators in 175
    employment 35
    Gross Domestic Product 29-30
    migrants in 32, 88, 98
    technology, new 49
    unemployment in 52, 62, 64-6
    urban population 84, 87
European Economic Community 30,
    38
expenditure *see* costs

family
    changes 77, 113, 152
    unemployment 65
financial institutions, international
    46
First World *see* industrialised
    countries
folk culture 18, 77-8, 86-7
France
    co-operatives in 66
    educators in 174
    employment in 35
    migrants in 88, 98, 174
    unemployment in 62, 66

urban population 87-8
Furtado, C. 55-6
future challenge 127-8

general and vocational education 122
geographical mobility 46-8
　see also mobility
Germany, Federal Republic of 35, 62, 98, 175
Gross Domestic and National Products see output
Gunder Frank, A. 69

high-income countries see industrial-ised
higher education 130-1, 136, 190
　access to 179
　in China and Japan 153, 157
　intercultural co-operation 129-40; and cultural identity 131-2; juridical and economic aspects 133-40; practical activities 132-3
history, meaning of 17-21, 137
hostility to migrants 99
human sciences and North-South relations 141-8

identity, cultural 19, 56, 131-2
ideology, crisis of 180-1
IDL see international division of labour
illiteracy 39, 119, 123
　new 74
　see also literacy
immigrants see migration; mobility
imports, educational 56, 145, 150-2, 156
　see also dependence; trade
independence 21, 26
India 29, 35
indigenisation 144, 145
industrialised countries
　choice in education 119
　culture 84, 96, 124
　emigration from 120
　higher education in 130-1, 136
　illiteracy in 123
　immigrants in 32, 37-8, 46, 63, 98-103, 135-6
　inequality in education 120-1
　international division of labour 25-44
　labour force 38

output 27-9, 30, 34-5
　relationships with developing countries 33-4, 46, 83; and human sciences 141-8; see also China and Japan
　research in 32, 38
　social services in 53
　technology, new 57-8
　unemployment in 62, 64-8
　urban population 84
　see also international market economies; planned economies
industry 50, 53-5
　new centres of 25, 27, 34-5
　see also output; technology
inequality in education 119-21
informal
　education 133-4, 180
　employment 38, 65, 68, 107
information 50-1, 124
initiatives, new 122-3
innovations 165, 168, 175
　see also new
institutionalization of research 142
institutions 18, 20, 99
intellectuals and working class 20
international/intercultural
　co-operation in education 190-4; creativity 160, 163-5; higher education 129-40; need for 125; technology, new 160, 162, 166, 167
　division of labour 25-44, 152-3
　exchange 77, 160-9; China and Japan 149-59
　institutions 99
　order of education, new 75
　production 55
　relations 45-6, 79
　see also migration; mobility
investment 39, 55, 156-7
Ireland 98
Italy 35, 62, 65, 67, 174

Japan 30, 35, 51, 62
　intercultural relations in China 149-59
Jeanson, F. 174
job creation see under employment
juridical aspects of higher education 133-40

Kiyoshi, K. 153
knowledge 54-5, 72

labour
  force 34-5; regulation of 153-4
  international division of 25-44,
    152-3
  market 107; segmentation 19, 38;
    transformation 10, 182
  see also employment; migration;
    mobility; work
language/s
  national 18
  problems 114-15
  voluntarist 141
Latin America 29, 35, 45, 84-5, 174
leaders, political 145
leisure
  changes 77
  culture and 89, 111-13
  employment dichotomy 72
  unemployment and 63
less developed countries *see*
  developing countries
liberation 7-9, 56
life, meaning of 17-21
lifelong education *see* education,
  lifelong
Ling Xing-Quang 153
linguistics *see* language/s
literacy 36, 56, 154
  see also illiteracy
low-income countries *see* developing
  countries
Luo, Y.Z. 155

manipulations 187-9
manual and mental labour, gap
  between 66
marginal countries *see* developing
  countries
marginalisation 20
Marinaleda co-operatives 64-5
market economies
  education in 36, 38
  higher education in 130-1, 136
  international economic relations
    45
  progressive teachers in 138
  unemployment in 62, 64-7
  see also industrialised countries
markets, new, need for 142-3
  see also labour market
mass and folk culture, rleationship
  between 86-7
mass media 18, 21, 41, 76, 89, 134
  see also communications

meaning of life and history 17-21
media *see* mass media
mental and manual labour, gap
  between 66
Mexico 174
microelectronics *see* computers;
  technology
middle class 63
Middle East 29-30, 35
migration 120
  creativities and 97-104
  culture and 88
  from developing countries 32,
    37-8, 46, 63, 98-103, 135-6
  from industrialised countries 120
  poor educational provision for
    135-6
  see also mobility
military *see* arms
minimal education 126
mobility, educational 109
mobility of capital 46
mobility of labour, technological
  changes
  cultural characteristics of work
    45
  democracy, industrial 53-4
  and economic crises 58
  employment creation 52-3
  geographical 46-8
  and information 50-1
  international relations 45-6
  knowledge and education 54-5
  professional 48-9
  and right to work 45-60
  technology: right to work 51-2;
    spread of 55-8
  unemployment 63
  work, organisation of 49-50
  worker education 71
  see also migration
models, changing 122-6
Mondragon co-operatives 64
more developed countries *see*
  industrialised countries
multinationals 31, 55
music 95

N'Dongo, S. 174
neo-colonialism 142, 145
Netherlands 98
networks 190-1
new
  colonialism 56

cultures 18-19
curricula, need for 110-11, 135-6,
    168
    educational: and cultural needs
        105-15; methods 77-8;
        policy and practice 76;
        structures and methods 77,
        78
    educators 77-8, 171, 173-5
    illiteracy 74
    initiatives 122-3
    jobs 39, 52-3, 55, 67-9, 119
    order, international 75
    policy goals 72
    technology *see* technology
    working class 73-6, 106
    world order and IDI 41-3
    see also change; innovation
newly industrialised countries *see*
    industrialised countries
non-formal *see* informal
non-market economies *see* planned
non-professional educators 173-5,
    179
North *see* industrialised countries
North America 30, 32, 35, 62, 84,
    87, 150

obstacles
    to change 123-4
    to lifelong education 181-4
Oceania 84
OECD countries 38
oil-exporting countries 36
opportunities and obstacles to
    lifelong education 178-89
    manipulations, creativities and
        prospects 187-9
    research issues 184-7
    trends 178-81
oppression 17, 143-4, 178
    see also domination
oral culture 111, 134
output 119, 149
    international comparisons 28-31
    see also industry
over-education 123-4

participation *see* community; trade
    unions
Peru 174
planned economies 36, 38, 45, 62-3,
    64
    see also industrialised countries

poetry 142
Poland 174
policy 178
    cultural 86-7
    educational and IDL 34-41, 76
    emerging educational and
        cultural needs 106-7
    employment 65-6, 68, 76
    new needs and goals 72
    right to work 101-2
    social instrument of 10-11
    for working class 106
    see also state
political
    de-colonisation 46
    independence 21
politics of migration 100
popular *see* folk
population and economy 29, 149
    in urban areas 84
practice, educational 11-12, 76
problems and changes 125-6
production system and worker
    education 71-6
    see also output
professional mobility 48-9
progress, lack of 109
progressive educators 137-8, 171,
    173-5
propaganda 56
prospects, lifelong education 187-9
provincialism 73
psychological problems 62, 65,
    68-9, 109

racism 143-4
re-appropriation of culture 18, 41
redistribution 161
refugees 98
regulations, educational 125
repression *see* domination;
    oppression
research 126-7
    cost of 145
    and development 31-2, 38, 40
    failings of 145-6
    on immigrants, need for 103
    institutionalisation of 142
    issues 184-7
    lack of relevance 114
    need for 103, 146
    powerlessness of researchers 141
resistance 124, 180, 183-4
resources 146

lack of 119-20
unutilized 171-2
results, educational 90-1
right
to education 120-1
to work 61, 101-2
rural areas and education 90-3, 155

savings 39
scarcity and inequality 119-20
scientific exchanges 149-59
see also technology
seasonal employment 66-7
Second World *see* planned economies
selection in China and Japan 153
self-instruction 78, 122
self-reliance 155-6
service industries 34-5
social
class *see* class
consciousness 144
relations 32-3
socio-cultural services, demand for 52-3
South *see* developing countries
South Africa 66
Spain 64-5, 89
sport 95, 112-13
'stabilisation programmes' 33-4
state
expenditure on education 119
and immigrants 102
and international division of labour 32-3
see also policy
stratification 113
see also class
structures, new educational 77
subcultures 63-4
Supek, R. 174
supply side factors and division of labour 153
surplus and inequality 119-20
Switzerland 98

teachers *see* educators
technological dynamics *see* economic
technology, new 49, 172
in China and Japan 156-7
in developing countries 55-6, 58
and education 54-5
and employment creation 51-3
and immigrants 57-8

and international co-operation 160, 162, 166-7
and mobility and development 50-2, 54
and right to work 51-2
spread of 55-8
training in 55, 107-8
and worker education 72-3
see also computers; industrialised countries
temporary employment 66
Third World *see* developing countries
trade, international 31, 33-4, 55, 150, 152
trade unions 53, 74, 102-3, 164
tradition 56
see also folk culture
training 38-40, 42
access to 101
in China and Japan 157
of educators 78, 160, 179
resources for 146
spread of 130
in new technology 55, 107-8
trends in lifelong education 178-81

underdeveloped countries *see* developing
underemployment 38, 63, 66-7
unemployment 38, 61-70
cost of 52
in developing countries 63, 66
education for 67-9
and family 65
of immigrants 101-2
in industrialised countries 62, 64-8
permanent 61
of young people 63-4, 101-2, 162
see also employment
United Kingdom 35, 52, 62, 66-7
United Nations 84
United States 30, 35, 62, 150
see also North America
universal right to education 120
unofficial *see* informal
unutilised human resources 171-2
Upper Volta 145-6
urban life 63, 83-90

values 68, 110
Varese, S. 174
vocational and general education

122
voluntarist language 141

wages, living without *see* unemploy-
    ment
Wajda, A. 174
Wallerstein, I. 69
war *see* arms industry
wealth, distribution of 50
West *see* industrialised countries
West Indies 175
Wiener, N. 50
women, employment of 63
work
    flight from 108
    organisation of 49-50
    relationships 108
    right to 61, 101
    see also employment; labour
workers' education 71-9, 154
    spaces, times, methods and
        techniques 76-9
    transformation of productive
        system and 71-6
working class 123-4
    in developing countries 39, 73-4
    and intellectuals 20
    new 73-6, 106
    policies for 106

young people
    and community development 95
    and employment policies 68
    and international co-operation
        161-3
    new demands of education
        110-11
    in rural areas 90
    unemployed 63-4, 101-2, 162
    and workers' education 71-9, 154
Yugoslavia 174

Zanier   L. 174